NEMEROV'S DOOR

NEMEROV'S DOOR

ESSAYS

ROBERT WRIGLEY

T|P

TUPELO PRESS
North Adams, Massachusetts

Nemerov's Door: Essays
Copyright © 2021 Robert Wrigley. All rights reserved.

Library of Congress Control Number: 2020949870
ISBN-13: 978-1-946482-50-1

Cover and text design by Howard Klein.

First paperback edition April 2021

Tupelo Press
P.O. Box 1767
North Adams, Massachusetts 01247
(413) 664-9611/Fax: (413) 664-9711
editor@tupelopress.org / www.tupelopress.org

Tupelo Press is an award-winning independent literary press that publishes fine fiction, non-fiction, and poetry in books that are a joy to hold as well as read. Tupelo Press is a registered 501(c)(3) non-profit organization, and we rely on public support to carry out our mission of publishing extraordinary work that may be outside the realm of the large commercial publishers. Financial donations are welcome and are tax deductible.

ART WORKS.
arts.gov

This project is supported in part by an award from the National Endowment for the Arts.

for my students
and in memory of Richard Hugo, Madeline DeFrees, and Clyde Fixmer

CONTENTS

INTRODUCTION

A number of these pieces began as lectures at writers' conferences; most were first, or eventually, published in literary journals. They were written over a period of thirty-odd years; a few have been revised but not a great deal. Most of them were like scratches at an itch having to do with poetic craft. I like seeing how poems work. I do not think, as William Carlos Williams did, that the poem is a "small (or large) machine made out of words." If the poem is a machine, it's a machine that more resembles a bird than an eggbeater. The poem seems to me more like a living thing; if it's a machine, it's a machine with a pulse. Several of the essays here are memoirs; the subjects of these I have occasionally addressed first in poems. There's a reason for that.

Now and then I have felt, over the decades during which I have written, the need to put down what my relationship has been to the art of poetry, or to a particular poem or poet. It's not like the need, or the impulse, to write a poem. Then again, it's not entirely different either. One of these essays *is* a poem. But nonfiction—these prose essays, that is—reports such information as its author, at least, believes or remembers to be true. A poem, on the other hand, serves the truth of its own making. Sure, the poem is written by the poet, but if everything is working as it should, the poem itself will have had a major role in its own creation. The poem, its language, and its form, exert extraordinary pressures on how the poet proceeds; they often tell the poet how to proceed. It's a curious (and from my point of view a blessed) fact that there are no binomial classifications of poetry, as there are in prose. The poem is not either fiction or nonfiction; it's a poem.

I should say that, as I have revised them and assembled them into this order, a few of the pieces included here have seemed strange to me now, especially in terms of tone, as though they were written by, or about, someone not me but who nevertheless clearly was me.

1

And clearly still is, albeit very much changed over the years. For years I was an angry young man, although I'm not sure I can say what it was I was angry about. Just being me was probably enough. Politics was always part of it too; I'd have to summon myself as a five-year-old in order to remember loving the republic unreservedly. But anger is energy, and it may have been the only source of energy I felt I possessed at that point in my life. Now I am over all that, the anger part. I certainly hope so. Then again, it's 2019; an amoral reality-TV huckster is president. I am as dismayed as I have ever been.

In any case, I didn't mean to become a poet. In my young man's life, I never read poems much, unless I had to for some course I was taking in school. The truth is, in those days I never felt much for poetry. It was less that it was difficult than that it struck me as uninteresting. All the formal matters—lines, stanzas, rhyme, meter, and more—seemed fussy and self-indulgent. But I dug language. I loved puns and word-play and wit. I wanted to do things with words. I meant to be a writer of some kind. A novelist, probably. What could be better than that? I was young. I didn't know much about anything, frankly. I had a lot to learn; I always will.

In a way, I could be called a product of what's referred to, pejoratively, as the "creative writing industry," by which is meant the matriculated academic study of literary writing—for the most part, the once relatively exotic and now ubiquitous—more recently the oft-maligned—MFA program. People who take the time to malign MFA programs make me weary, especially the ones who argue that they're fighting for standards or protecting the integrity of literature. Literature doesn't need their help. It's fine. Always has been. And you couldn't kill poetry with a meat cleaver. Lots of people believe they want to write poems and therefore they try. Most of them do not succeed.

In 1981, in Seattle, at the annual Associated Writing Programs conference (so few people they nearly all fit in one modest-sized hotel), I listened to someone in the audience carp to a panel of well-known poets about all the "wannabes" studying in such programs. The panelists sat there a moment, silent. Then James Tate said, "Look, man, they're not hurting anybody." The number of MFAs granted in a year nationwide is dwarfed by the number of MBAs. According to something called the Graduate Management Admission Council, there are more than 100,000 MBAs awarded each year in the United States. Whether they serve the nation or the world better than MFAs is open to debate.

It should not come as a surprise to you to hear that an MFA does not make you a poet; it makes you a person who holds the MFA degree. By itself, the MFA is an academic credential that may allow you to find a job teaching an enormous load of classes for shitty money and no benefits. In addition, there's not much you learn in an MFA program that you can't also learn on your own. But you learn it faster in a program, usually much faster, and you learn, along the way, how to be very efficient in accumulating the tools you will need to write. And if you pick them up, you'll need them. It's best to have them all, even the ones you use only once. And by the way, there are no rules. This is why you have to know them all.

Once upon a time, as a twenty-one year old undergraduate student, I took a class in writing poetry and the art of poetry took me. It was as though I'd been walking past the cathedral of poetry for years, and then, on a whim, or by some stroke of recklessness and what-the-hell, I went inside. And lo, everything changed. I began to try to write poems, and it changed the way I lived. Once I started writing poems, I never stopped. I couldn't. Now it's impossible for me to imagine not writing poems, although that could change. In addition to time, it requires a lot of energy and stamina. You've got to stay nimble in as many ways as you can. I suspect that writing and reading give me a lot of what energy, stamina, and nimbleness I still possess at sixty-eight.

Several of these pieces, therefore, speak in some way of my coming to poetry. There really isn't a whole lot to it. I took that class and within the first twenty minutes I was not merely interested, I was fascinated; I was hooked, and I have never stopped being so. The particular poets whose work I write about here—Dickey, Hugo, Knight, Nemerov, Plath, and Robinson—were poets I first encountered along my way as an aspiring poet, and they were among the poets who set me on the course I have traveled ever since. They are far from the only ones; they're just the ones I've written about. I am still, and I always will be, a student of poetry. If you think you want to write poems, there's something you should know: no matter how long you do it, it never gets any easier. And that's not a bad thing either, not at all.

It's also true that I would probably not have written any of this as prose if I had not, in the same nearly forty years, been a teacher. I might still have been a poet, if I'd worked in advertising or been a carpenter. But the poems I offer commentary upon here are poems I have taught, and it was in the teaching of those poems that I came to grips with the artistry, and the workmanship, in them. For those opportunities, I am grateful to the colleges and universities that have employed me, but I am far more grateful to the students.

Most students in poetry writing classes do not become—or do not stay—poets, even the graduate students, who at the time probably believed it was their life's calling. I have always told them, writing is the easiest thing in the world not to do. Nothing in the daily life you live requires you to write poems, but something about your life—if you are indeed to follow through and keep writing poems—goes unlived if you don't. And when you choose to write poems, you are entering into a conversation with all the poets before you and among you. Poets after you will continue the conversation. It's a way to see the world, to be in the world. It's a way to live, and it's all-encompassing. You learn to think like a poet. Your eyes are open in a way that has something to do with the need to say what it is you have seen or experienced or imagined (or, most often, all of the above). You need to make things connect. Your ears are attuned to the music of the language, and you begin to understand that musical descriptions are often the most accurate. Students talk to me about their lives, and very often, at some point, I stop them and ask, "Have you written that poem?" Mostly they haven't, but often, afterward, they will. Some people think there are too many poets and too many poems, and that's bullshit. Imagine a world in which there are perceived to be too many dancers, too many musicians, too many songs.

It's hard to write poems. Certainly it's very hard to write good poems. And the more you read, the more you understand how unlikely it is that you have ever written a good poem or, for that matter, that you ever will again. And great poems? Every time you sit down with pencil and paper or at a keyboard, greatness is what you should aspire to. The fact that this is not probable does not discourage you. As a matter of fact, the difficulty—and the improbability—is the fuel that drives you. Failure, repeatedly, turns out to be an excellent goad. "Fail again," said Samuel Beckett. "Fail better."

My former teacher, Richard Hugo, once wrote a slender book of essays called *The Triggering Town*. There's no other book like it. No one else has ever spoken of writing poetry with such clarity and frankness, nor in such a fiercely personal and non-academic tone. I don't know if it's true or not, but I have heard (from his late widow, Ripley) that *The Triggering Town* has sold more copies than all of Hugo's books of poems combined, and that makes me sad, in a way. Everything Hugo says in that book is enacted, demonstrated, and made abundantly clear in the poems themselves. (He always said, "I only know one way to write, and that's the way I do it. But you can't write like me. You'll have to find your own way." Some of Hugo's students did that; many others did not.) If *The Triggering Town* has indeed sold more copies than all of Hugo's books of poems combined, it probably says more about peoples' dreams than about their love of poetry or their thirst for some kind of self-expression. They want to *be* poets.

I understand that. There were a few years early on when, if I am honest, I actually preferred being a poet to writing a poem. That is, I preferred having written a poem to writing one. I liked reading the "finished product" and I liked letting it confirm for me my own . . . *genius* (we're human; we all do it). But somewhere along the way that changed too. I began to prefer writing to having written. I learned to value the process more than the product. Sometimes people ask me, "What are your favorites of your own poems?" I won't lie. Pressed, I will confess that I do have favorites among those that are out in the world in books. But I always answer the same way, and I am being honest when I say so. "The next one I write," I reply.

Which is for me the drawback about such a collection as this. I've spent many, many hours working on these essays, and I could have been writing poems instead. I always get that feeling when I write prose; I'm feeling it a bit right now. There are only a few things I sometimes prefer doing to putting words on paper, in lines.

Finally, I must thank my wife, Kim Barnes, who is a superlative writer of prose—memoirs, novels, essays, and stories (she began her writing life as a poet). A reviewer once said of her, "Barnes is incapable of writing a bad sentence," and as I've driven myself through this mostly all-the-way-from-one-side-of-the-page-to-the-other collection of essays, that bit of highly accurate praise has occurred to me repeatedly. Kim has read this collection, and any bad sentences herein she let pass in kindness to me.

Moscow Mountain, Idaho, April 2019

THE WEIGHT OF ARRIVAL

This was in Ohio, in the mid-1980s, on something called the Ohio Poetry Circuit.

"Where do you get your ideas for poems?" a young man asked me. It was the third or fourth question-and-answer session I'd done in as many days, at as many colleges, and this was the third or fourth time I'd heard some form of that particular question. It's a common one, asked most often by respectful but usually uninitiated people.

"What ideas?" I said. "Where?"

The young man sort of flinched. What exactly had he accused me of, he must have wondered? And what was I accusing him of in response?

My explanation that day in Ohio was necessarily brief but nevertheless honest.

My intent here is to offer a more thoughtful, detailed, and hopefully helpful answer. I want to talk about the process, the movement from trigger to truth, from seed to blossom, from delight to wisdom, focusing, in this case, on the early stages, on the beginnings of what I know as poems.

As I said that day, rarely, in my own experience, does a poem grow from the seed of an idea. It's writing; semantic distinctions are critical. At its most general, the word "idea" means everything our minds take note of and nothing in particular. There's a kind of dull reality to some ideas: my computer's cursor pulsing just now—does my taking note of it elevate it to the status of idea, or is it just a bit of information taken in? sensory datum? Of course, by using the verb "pulsing," I've given it a kind of metaphorical life. Does that make it more like an idea?

The other day I had to move a few tons of rock unearthed in a building project. I hauled wheelbarrow after wheelbarrow load down the path from the yard to the garden, then dumped them over the edge into what we call "the thicket," a little side canyon between us and the river. It's steep there, and some of the rocks tumbled only a few feet then stopped against a stalk of sumac. But others rolled like mad, crashing into the underbrush, the syringa and cottonwood and elderberry: sometimes the rocks themselves were no longer visible, but I could chart their progress by the disturbances at the top of the thicket's canopy. The beginnings of poems are, if you're lucky, like that second kind of rock: things you watch and worry, see and re-see from some other angle. Whatever the tensions that energize the poem as finished product, the things we perceive as readers are one thing—the served-up, well-risen soufflé—whereas the "idea" that generated the poem is often as simple and elementary as an egg. In my experience, the generating "idea" is often absent completely from the finished poem.

I get my ideas, if they may be called that, from my body, or my body's personality and aura, from my brain, that is, which is also my body's hard drive. Much more often than not I begin with a phrase, an image, a particular verbal—or aural—picture. Rarely ever do I begin a poem with the end in mind, or with some notion of what the poem will be *about*. Aristotle called the idea the "form, or form-giving cause," and I like the word "cause" much more than I like "idea." It is easier for me to go back and explain what "caused" this or that poem I have written, much easier than it would be to get at the idea behind it. And very often, reducing a poem to its "main idea," or even to the seed of the idea it came from, merely waters the whole thing down. It's like being told that "Stopping By Woods On a Snowy Evening" is a poem about death.

I'm making a distinction between what the body apprehends

and what the brain processes into a product of its own invention through language and form. That product will come only with work; language and the formal requirements of poetry are how we refine what we sense into things we can know in useful ways, which is to say, understand. The poem is not the sum of the mind's chaws and whittlings. No truly literary writing is. The poem is the offspring of a kind of human totality, what the language enables poets to be, and to do, if they bring to the endeavor the body, the brain, and the holy ghost of it all, the imagination.

Though "imagination" has as its root the word image, the thing itself—that quality of invention and discovery—is an abstraction. To "imagine" something is to conjure to the mind's eye, ear, skin, tongue, or nose a portrait of that thing, vaporous but personally accurate, tempered by memory as much as by novelty. The imagination does not exist as we know it without the senses or the memory of them. No matter how deranged the senses are, their measurements and apprehensions are still sensory. Of the body. Bodiless poets don't have a lot to say.

For a poet, the image, or the musical phrase, can cause all sorts of things to happen. The sway of a field of grass in the wind might summon up the invisible, stroking hand of God, though just as easily, and not incidentally, what comes forth may be the sweet tongue-and-lip-driven, sibilant motion of "sway," which in turn might lead—thanks to the ear's relentless inclination toward rhyme—to "pray," or "prey." The engine of poetry runs on a mixture of processed sensory data and unfettered music. Now one, now the other, now both. The world is awash with poems that are in fact schematic diagrams of their own enactments. From object to object, from phrase to phrase, rhyme to rhyme, tick and murmur, the progression is logical or intuitive or both. Poems don't come from ideas so much as they dramatize their own development. Donald Hall, speaking of his life as a reader of poems, said, "Trust the poem, not the poet." I would argue that the same advice applies just as much to the poet writing as to the reader. Reading—really reading—a poem is like watching a time-lapse film of a flower's blossoming. It's not a lot different for the poet in the act of writing. The decisions the poet makes are not willed upon the poem but are the result of the poet listening to the poem's own aspirations.

I'm speaking primarily of lyric poetry. Or meditative, associative. I am, but not exclusively. The narrative poem is obligated to a plot. Something happens and keeps on happening, or other somethings ensue, likewise happening. There is exposition, rising action, a crisis, a denouement. The narrative poem tells a story but that story may often be as spontaneous and unforeseen as the music or the accretion of imagery, and the plot may be as often guided by sound and sensory connection as by any predetermined conclusion. The sound of sparrows' wings as the birds threaded their ways through a blackberry bramble—"little breathy drums," I called them, "damning and damning." The sound of those wings, and the sound of the words set forth in the creation of it (from "drums" to "damning" seems obvious to me now), leads, logically and sensibly, to what it was that "drew me on," an old car swallowed by thorny canes and inhabited by a pair of human skeletons. When people ask me after readings where it was I found that old car, I must admit I'm pleased. Usually I grin and tap my index finger between my ear and my forehead. Imagination and music, I mean, though I'm not sure they're two things at all, but one.

The primary struggle in writing is toward unity, a striving toward something like understanding, though the best poems are not, I believe, the ones we "understand," but the ones we recognize as true, the ones that we feel possess us with their utter rightness, even if that rightness is otherwise beyond our explanation. It is a truth we feel far more than we can describe or even envision; certainly we may feel it more than we understand it. And of course it's entirely reasonable that we should wonder about the origin of such a thing as the whole, unified creation. It's entirely reasonable that we should wonder at the glimpse the poet must have begun with, and how it compares to the view we are left with. What that young man wanted to know those years ago was simply a way of feeling. He wanted to sense the pulse, the blood that moved the poems toward life. But I should remember *how* he asked his question. "*Where,*" he said, "do you get your ideas for poems?" He meant location; he wanted a map to an imaginary world. And here, tapping my finger against the side of my head is not quite sufficient. I mean the air too, as well as the vessel, the body dreaming itself into the real world its brain imagines in words.

I don't think there's anything mysterious about where poems come from, nor anything magical, really, about their writing. What *is* magical and full of mystery is the finished poem itself. (Paul Valery insisted that "poems are never finished, only abandoned," and that is also very true.) What poets love most is the feeling that comes from entering into the work, the movement towards and then into and through the poem. It's a kind of fierce concentration; it's also a kind of nutshell oblivion the poet cultivates. It's a trance not unlike the trance of the ditch-digger or the mountain climber, where the shovel meets the soil, fissure accommodates the foot, pencil nuzzles paper.

It's true, I'm talking about inspiration.

Inspiration, that old bugaboo and burdensome misconception. That young man didn't ask where I got my *inspiration* for poems, although many others have. I'm feeling reckless here. To admit that one believes in something called inspiration is almost foolish or quaint, like confessing a faith in Santa Claus or the wisdom of the Electoral College. In his autobiography, Thomas Edison claimed "genius is one percent inspiration and ninety-nine percent perspiration," and that

13

seems so accurate a pronouncement we simply nod and agree. Dick Hugo liked to tell the story of when a gallery fan asked Arnold Palmer if that last shot wasn't at least a little bit lucky, and Palmer responded, "Yes, but I find that the more I practice, the luckier I get."

The inspiration I'm talking about is not something that happens to you; it's not a bolt of lightning or the tap of the Muse's fingertip. It's hard work and it's the willingness to fail repeatedly on the way. It's something you find your way into. It's a way of getting lost in the woods on purpose, walking head down but intently, taking in the array of soil and stump and lichen and vine. (Sometimes it's more like crawling.) Only the forest here is words and syllables, the slopes and gullies are cadence and phrase. It's a long walk sometimes. It takes receptivity and sweat. Practice and perspiration, and a kind of reckless fearlessness. But you get lost inside the language itself, until there is a point at which it is no longer clear whether you are wielding the words or the words are wielding you. Sometimes simply becoming aware of that conundrum makes the woods disappear. Sometimes a man from Porlock arrives. Or calls. Or sends a text.

The process of writing a poem is, as many know, a making as much as a creating. The derivation of the word "poet" is from *poietes*, Greek, "to make." For years, before my mother went to work in order to "make money," she made our clothes and our meals; in the language of domesticity, she made our home. My father, with his array of gleaming tools, could make just about anything. I remember getting up late at night, thirsty or needing to pee, and wandering through the house, following some dim glow to its source—my mother at her Singer sewing machine. Sometimes I could stand there quite a while, peering up under the light of the machine as it whirred, before her concentration was broken and she took me in hand and walked me back to bed. In the basement, my father's workbench was altar and pulpit and organ, and I used to watch him at work for hours, sole parishioner in the church of artful and practical manufacture. I could be silent for long periods then.

"Now we're getting somewhere," they said, each to no one, to themselves.

That's the idea. To get somewhere, from where the poem begins to where it arrives. And that reminds me how much I love Stephen Mitchell's beautiful translation of Rilke's poem "The Spanish Trilogy." At the very least the opening section of that poem strikes me as a plaintive invocation, a passionate longing, a prayer that he might "make the Thing, Lord Lord Lord, the Thing." And isn't the Thing—in this case more ephemeral than any shirt and less apparently practical than any box or shelf—isn't the Thing the poem? It is made from everything that is available, "from so much that is uncertain and from me, / from me alone and from what I do not know." Wood, cloth, words. And there it is, rudimentary, in need of buttons, hinges, locks, polish, or revision.

From the clouds and from the stars. From the words and the way the words jostle and touch, the Thing, the poem, which, in Rilke's words, "weighs nothing but arrival."

The language "weighs nothing," and for me language is itself an "idea," and the source of many others. Idea. From the Greek again, *idein*, "to see." Language is how we process what we think and feel, and how we know what we see. To come into possession of the language is to find it inseparable from the actual world it represents. Outside my window now, that tall, intermittently conical green thing—a yellow pine tree. Tree. First the language was all sound, a word the tiniest of songs, an itty-bitty ballad whose story we agreed to. Someone somewhere along the way said it and it was, and we have been saying and recognizing and making ever since. And if there is nothing new under the sun, there are still innumerable ways of seeing, seven-plus billion perceptions and perspectives. It is the poet's challenge to say what is said in such a way that what is being stated, no matter how familiar it might be, is new and unheard of. Or else immediately and strangely known. When a writer makes such a thing happen on the page, the result is often called "inspired."

My youngest son, when he was four maybe, found during a walk along the river the tail feather of a redtail hawk: deep orange going red, white strokes, black bottom barbs, and a boutonniere of tangly down near the bottom. He was thrilled and turned to show me.

"Look, Daddy!" he called. "It's a . . . a . . . it's—". In his sudden joy, with his modest vocabulary, he was struggling for the right word.

"It's a *bird-leaf!*" he cried.

I was so grateful to him just then. I thought for sure that he'd handed me the beginning, the seed, the perfect idea for a poem. But I was wrong. I've put in hours and filled pages trying to make that poem, but so far nothing I've written can equal the pure rightness of his simple saying. His wrong word was inspired that day, and his inspiration inspired me as auditor, as hearer. His reader. His bird-leaf is a kenning, like whale-road for the sea or like wound-hoe for a sword. A simple compound word that is a metaphor, a tiny perfect poem.

It was later the same day, when I entered the living room to find him lying on his back, tilting back and forth the tiny plastic hourglass from a Boggle game.

"You know what this stuff is in here, Daddy?" he asked, speaking of the white grit inside.

"What?" I asked.

"It's time-sugar."

It's easy, sometimes, to get nostalgic about the days when poetry was purely an oral art. It was of necessity more memorable then, or at least *easier* to remember. My son's accidental and perfect metaphors look more like what might be called traditional (or mythical) inspiration because they are so purely vocal and spontaneous, so not-composed. They were brought forth fully formed from the mouth of a babe. Or from the muse. Poetry in its earlier days might also have seemed— what?—more organic, more spontaneous, more natural. Bardic. Less composed, less self-consciously constructed, less a work of artifice. Or else, with its heavier rhythms and signal rhymes so much in the service of memorability, it now seems, on the other hand, more contrived and ritualistic. It's neither and it's both. It is poetry, and the thing itself is vaster than all its procedures. The poem is the sum, and the sum is more than lines, tropes, and parts. What is inspired about a poem may be a particular image or rhetorical approach, or else it may be simply the poem's totality—the way it lives on and beyond the page, the way it breathes. "Inspiration," aside from its theological connotations, means simply breathing, the taking in of air.

I would have been twelve or thirteen when I saw *Dr. Zhivago* in a movie theatre in St. Louis with my parents and my sister. And when Omar Sharif's Zhivago, warming his hands over a candle, set pen to paper, and the camera cut back to Julie Christie's Lara still curled warm and gorgeous in bed, I believed in several kinds of inspiration at once. Writing was a way you could be more alive. When I first started writing poems, I tried to do it standing up, at a manual portable typewriter on a dresser. The fact is, I couldn't sit down. And still I spent a lot of time waiting. I would have known about the traditional invocation of the muse, but I can't remember trying it myself. "Come on," I might have murmured, swaying a little—my body trying to show me it was like a dance.

It's not embarrassing, this memory. I'm fond of that young man I was, standing there, wishing and hoping at least as much as he worked. The work would pull him on, though the wishing and hoping were part of it too. I believe they all lead to a kind of seat-of-the-pants ingenuity. I experimented and imitated. I was acquiring a measure of dexterity with the tools I naively thought I already possessed. I was finding my way mapless into the poem's dark woods; I was breathing-in the language, falling under its spirit, its spell, learning to let the poem be its own inspiration, and thus my own.

The inspiration I speak of cannot be taught, though I believe it can be learned. It is the one-percent solution, Edison's "genius"; it is sweat and more sweat and more often than not failure. It takes inordinate practice and cultivated luck. The idea for the poem is what you carry into the forest, or it is what you find there, and it is what allows the poem to become; it is cause, while the poem is effect. The beginning is the first step, the first word, the first line; the poem is destination, not quite inevitable and as unpredictable as tomorrow, which is everywhere and anywhere and, like the poem, weighs nothing but arrival.

SEEING ARROWHEAD, SEEING FLINT

You have to have an eye for what you hunt; your vision must be attuned. Almost all the world is camouflage, and even what isn't is often meant to draw us away from what's hidden and trying to stay that way. I was hunting chukar partridges once, along the breaks of the lower Salmon River, not far from Riggins, Idaho. I'd been climbing up a rugged, cheatgrass-infested slope for probably 600 or 800 vertical feet, and I was wheezing from the effort. I could hear my heart. My shotgun felt as heavy as a manhole cover, and though it was very cool, the sweat ran down my forehead and burned my eyes, just as I crested a knob, a false summit halfway up the ridge from the river. I stopped to rest, to catch my breath, and that's when I noticed, across a narrow sage-clotted swale, that the ground opposite of where I stood appeared to be moving. It looked as though it were migrating right up the slope and out from under its vegetation.

I blinked. Chukars. A covey of them, a flock on the ground. They were running, and when I swung the shotgun up they exploded into flight, reversed direction, and were gone before I'd even tightened my finger over the trigger. I'd been there on that hump of land, not five yards away, for seven or eight seconds before I saw them going, or before I understood what I saw.

And I remember crouching with a friend outside his pickup, as he whispered to me and pointed. "Ten o'clock from that red stand of sumac there, a buck and two does." He was pointing and I could see the bloody smear of the sumac, but that was all. I didn't want to admit I couldn't see the deer. And then suddenly I could see them. They seemed to melt into place, to shimmer into being, to emerge from the background.

"Right," I said, "I see them," and I must have looked away then, maybe at him, to acknowledge my thanks, because then I couldn't find them again, until it seemed to me that I quit looking, until I quit imposing what I assumed I knew to be there and simply saw what I saw. A whitetail buck, elegantly and symmetrically racked; not two does but four, in fact, and the white flag of a fifth—the buck's most skittish mate—moving off up the slope, two o'clock. West.

It was my youngest son, a few summers ago, who spotted the snake between our friend BJ's feet. We'd been on a long walk in the mountains and now we were just standing there, resting, looking out over a soggy meadow of tussocks and witchgrass.

"BJ!" Jace yelled. "There's a snake!"

Our children were raised in serious rattlesnake country, so they've grown up with a hyper-developed snake sense. They never reach under anything without looking first, and they watch where they're walking.

This was just a common northwestern garter snake though. Harmless. BJ even tried to pick it up, but it slithered away into the marsh grass and hummocks. You could catch a brown, stripy glimpse of it for the first foot or two, then it was gone, there but not there, invisible in its earthly world.

"Wow," Jace said. "It's gone." He stayed behind a while though, looking, when we walked on.

"How do you see so much in a poem?" a freshman asked me once. He wasn't arguing that what I saw wasn't there but that he had not seen it and felt he would never have seen it, that he would never have the eye for it, this extremely close poetry-reading thing, unless someone were there, pointing things out to him.

William Stafford said the poem was something "you see from the corner of your eye," and that's true for the poem's reading and its writing as well. For how long, how many times, must Michelangelo have circled that block of perfect white marble before the shape of the *Pieta* began to emerge in his mind's eye. Like the deer, the chukar, the agate among the stones along a beach. It's not just seeing but a vision, not seeing more than is there but all that might be.

Pick a sense, any sense. A palate and tongue for wine; the birder's momentary unraveling of the most elaborate and similar of warblers' songs. Imagine my great-grandfather, blinded by cataracts after years in the coal mines, now in the cool dark of his room, the radio playing baseball from St. Louis and him reading with his old blunt fingertips bill after bill as he amazed my father and uncle—"this is a five, twenty, a one, a ten." He never missed: no braille but ink, I guess. When I asked, he said he didn't know how he did it, only that he could. I had another student, a .400-plus hitter who, when I asked what it was like to hit that well, cocked his head, took a deep breath and thought for a few seconds, then said, "Well, the ball's just really big and slow. You can see it so well you almost can't miss it."

I lived with my wife and children for a decade in the canyon of the Clearwater River, in north central Idaho. It was a wild and dramatic place. The world there was like a huge room in the house. The canyon everywhere outside the windows made that too-small house seem livably large. It was like abiding in a 10,000-acre palace. We had blinds, but we used them only to keep out the summer sun. Mostly we preferred being able to see. Being inside the house seemed like just another way of being out in the air and the wind, the smells and sounds of that particular speck of the earth's surface. And the canyon, as well as the river, was the essence of everything. It was the logic of everywhere else on the way to where we were. Even the most geologically myopic could see how everything had always moved down with the rain and snow melt to where the water was and wasn't, always there and always going away. That was the miracle of the river you could see, what Heraclitus attempted to encapsulate with his famous paradox: you cannot, he suggested, cross the same river twice. How obvious and how obviously wrong. I think of the wise and wonderful people I have known who live along the river, and who would have surely shaken their heads and wondered what sort of fool that old Greek must have been.

Come summer, once or twice, in July most often, we went down to the river and walked upstream to where a massive braid of slow but constant spring creeks fed down the canyon wall through a five-acre bramble of blackberries. There, not far from a sand beach and a shallow back eddy filled with flotsam from the most recent floods—the hood of a vintage VW Beetle; an old rocking horse un-tacked from its springs and frame and now broken-necked and filled with sand; a chunk of eaves, its tar paper and asphalt shingles waving in the current—we would spread out and begin, all four of us, to thumb through the bottomless churn of gravel and sand, looking for slivers of flint, looking for chips, shards, man-made fractures, but mostly looking for arrowheads.

They're hard to find but not impossible, arrowheads. Across the river from where we hunted is a place, a highway rest stop now, where archeologists have unearthed evidence of 10,000 years of hu-man habitation, and for all but the last 300 or so the people who have lived there used all sorts of shaped and sharpened stone tools. They gutted fish and skinned game with stone knives. They used bows and arrows to hunt with and make war with and defend themselves from attack with, and for all that time they used the good stones here, the hard, chippable flints, to fashion their arrowheads and tools. Here was their armory, their powder magazine; here also was their kitchen, their grocery, their machine shop, their amazing nightly skylight. Here was their big house.

You sift and lift and turn the stones, and sometimes you find dozens of chips. That's all you find, for the most part: the evidence of centuries of making arrowheads, not arrowheads themselves. Chips look like that which has been tapped away, all the parts of the stone that are not the actual point itself, pieces of the greater mold. Sometimes you find a chip that looks like part of an arrowhead's shadow. It's as though you'd come across a chunk of marble that had once held the lip of Michelangelo's dead Jesus.

It was a friend of ours who started us hunting arrowheads on the river. He and his wife once lived at our place for a year while we were gone. He had the eye for it. He walked down the river once and found what had obviously been a perfect start, a beautifully tapered, large point, one notch of which already roughed in, but the other side, where the opposite notch would have been, gone. Imagine, he urged. Hours of tapping, with an awl of obsidian and a mallet of elkhorn, then *clink*. You wonder, my friend said, what that culture's word might have been for such extreme exasperation and disappointment, and if, on a sunny day just like this one, it might not have echoed a good half-mile up and down the canyon. A single, agonized, and outraged syllable. Or maybe not. A sigh. Start over.

None of us knew that it was illegal to hunt for arrowheads, or if not to hunt for them, then to keep them.

One day our friend and his wife had been hunting for a couple of hours when a man approached. It's not an easy place to walk there, along the shore. You have to scramble over nests of deadfall snags and beaver dams; you have to circumnavigate vivid green stands of poison ivy and climb over and around blade-edged boulders of fractured basalt. It was a place you went on purpose, not just for a stroll. You had to want to get there. And here he was, this stranger. He made small talk with my friends for a few minutes, speaking of the river and of fishing, and when my friend's wife held up her palm to show him what she'd found—a small, reddish, perfect arrowhead—the man looked away instead, out over the current toward the rest stop on the other side. He stared out.

"You know, it's against the law to keep arrowheads if you find any," he said, after a second. My friend's wife slowly folded her fingers back around the arrowhead. "Maybe what you're hunting for is flint."

The three of them made a bit more small talk and the man left. That day, in addition to the one his wife found, my friend picked up three perfect arrowheads, and then something came down on him. Something weird and spirit-connected, a chill and a flush, equal parts guilt and fear and something unnameable. This was not a man frightened of the law. What he felt was something else. He closed his eyes then and said to himself a few simple words, not exactly a prayer. A thanks. Then he tossed all three points back to the river and shore, and he and his wife went home. She kept her arrowhead, though. It was her first, her only one. The visitor's looking away, she thought: was that tacit permission? And who was he? What was that all about? It was just the one, after all, only her, only this one. How many must there be, buried in the sand and gravel for thousands of years?

It turned out that it was impossible for me not to covet the arrowheads my friends had found. I was the one who lived there, and I loved the place. I used to go out every night, last thing before bed, no matter what time it was, no matter what the weather, just so I could stand on the deck and watch and listen to the river, smell the canyon smells—sage, syringa, cottonwood, dust. I wanted to memorize the shadows the moonlight cast. I wanted to connect myself to the place where I lived as much as I could, and I wanted such a thing out of time in my hand—an arrowhead of my own. I wanted to reach back into the history of the place and touch the maker's hand.

My keen-eyed friend came for a visit and took a walk with me one day, to a beach a mile or so downstream from the house. We had been standing there, looking out at the river for a minute or so—looking at a river, that thing you almost can't help doing; it's like looking into a campfire after dark—when he reached down and plucked from the mud right in front of me, almost between the toes of my shoes, a small perfect arrowhead the color of coffee with cream. That he gave it to me was an act of great generosity, I think, and I treasure that arrowhead still. But I cursed myself for looking out, not down. Why was I always looking for something distant, when what I wanted was here, under my feet, between my toes?

Still, I wanted to find my own arrowhead. I wanted to pick one up from among a million similar stones. I wanted to be the first person to touch it since the maker dropped it or the shooter lost it. It had to do with the idea of place and of home, and more than ever in my life I wanted to be home. Home where I did my life's work.

For reasons I will soon describe, I no longer hunt for arrowheads, but I'm still fascinated by them. As much as anything else about the arrowhead as object, I was and am thunderstruck by the patience it must have taken to work a chunk of rock into a useful tool. Were there people whose tribal and cultural specialty was the making of arrowheads? In a way, I have known for most of my life that making, the making of anything worthwhile, is a function of patience. Whether it's making a baseball break or driving it into the gap for extra bases, reading or writing a poem, you have to wait for it. You have to let it show itself to you. The people who made arrowheads were obligated to make them as though their lives depended on them, because, of course, their lives did depend on arrowheads. Is that a skill too? That patience? Or that driven necessity? A stone and a stone and a bludgeon of antler or branch: this is about life.

Somehow—I don't really know how—I wanted to live that way. I wanted to make something that mattered. Not an arrowhead, but something the arrowhead was analogous to. Small, beautiful, and useful. And somehow maybe even deadly. Like a poem.

I used to think I might try to make an arrowhead myself. I'd consider a rock to sit on, a slab of basalt smooth enough to be almost

25

comfortable, maybe with a good, gradually-opening fracture I might use as a kind of vise, to hold the flint as I worked it. But that's all I ever did, was think about it. It is the sort of romanticism of which I seem endlessly capable. Though I kill and eat the occasional bird or fish, I use steel hooks and factory-made shotgun shells, not to mention graphite fishing rods and guns the hard metal parts of which have been machined to minute tolerances the naked eye cannot see. Most of my food comes from corporations that raise, process, package, transport, and retail their product to me and my fellow citizens as though it were magic. Unless I'm camping, the fire that cooks my meat comes through electrical wires or courses through copper wire from a propane tank. It's old news. I'm cut off from the earth and its rhythms, I'm less alive than I wish I were. I'm seeing the wrong things, not what matters.

Or so it seems.

When I first began looking for arrowheads I found that I could cover fairly large tracts of potential hunting ground in relatively brief periods of time. In the course of an hour or so I might find a good fistful of interesting and sometimes beautiful shards, clearly "worked," shaped, that is, by human intent and not the earth's or the river's haphazard hammer. The first few times, which is to say the first year or so, that I hunted, I began with a sense of determination and urgency that quickly sagged into a desultory scratch and probe. I'd find myself watching the way the river moved or eyeing a great blue heron's slow stalk after a crawdad. Near the end of it, I was just bored.

It was like picking huckleberries, only the exact reverse. Huckleberrying usually gets boring because there are so many berries; they're everywhere, and you start passing up the smaller ones, going from bush to bush after bigger and more swollen fruits until you've crawled a quarter-mile from where you started. You look up dizzy and amazed, but you're rich with berries. On the shore of the river, I'd search a space perhaps a square yard-and-a-half large, attempting to peel back the skin of the shore layer by thin layer. I'd lay the occasional handsome chip on a driftwood log and keep going, and when I looked up at last the same dizzy amazement was there, but I'd have little to show for it other than gritty fingers.

And then one day, I found a chunk, a big chunk, of what could have been a spear point or maybe the last inch and a half of a stone knife, a sort of rounded, sharp sticking end, and the whole thing almost perfectly symmetrical in color—white on one side, near purple on the other—ending in an all-wrong break. My heart raced. I could feel a kind of high come on and a kind of sourceless clarity too. I'd pretty much given up that day. I was just diddling, looking for a few more interesting shards, enough, say, to fill a jelly jar on the mantle, a little currency of conversation pieces maybe. I was just flicking, just lightly dusting, using my right index finger. When the chunk showed itself, it was as though it had been there all along. It had been, of course. I almost didn't pick it up at first; I was sure I'd already looked it over and tossed it aside. But seeing it was like examining one of those strange, computer-generated illustrations in which the illusion of a three-dimensional hummingbird or peace sign emerges from a mass of color and line, at just the moment you feel yourself going almost wall-eyed from the impenetrable sameness.

It was, I guess, Zen-like. When I quit looking for the deer across the way, the deer presented themselves to me; one day I quit trying to write poems and began allowing them to emerge from the language and the imagination almost on their own. The point I found that day carried me a year or more. But eventually its incompleteness lessened its vitality for me. It was, I began to see, not much more than a factory reject, something tossed away, or, because it was broken, junked. A draft. Something the river swept away and swept back up centuries later. And I wondered about the rightness of it, I admit. I fretted over the propriety of taking possession of a thing that is, in fact, an archaeological artifact, the record of an ancient people's daily living. It seemed like an invasion of their privacy. I loved looking still, but as I probed and dusted and flicked, I wanted as much as ever to find what I was looking for and felt almost worried that I might.

A neighbor from those days, a man in his eighties, said people used to come to the other side of the river, where the rest stop is now, and head down to the beach with backhoes and large shake-boxes and sieves. They'd spend whole days digging up stone and sand in search of arrowheads, axes, beads made of bone, Stone Age relics. My neighbor and I lived on what had once been native land. We were still on the reservation, and we were both white.

"That was bad, the way they went after them things," he said. "It had to be stopped. Now if you find an arrowhead down there, it ain't going to hurt nothin' if you keep it. What good would it do to leave it there?"

"You ever find an arrowhead?" I asked.

"Lord, yes. Lots. Don't know what ever happened to them though. Boys give them away at school maybe. Or they got threw away."

We'd be leaning on his fence and, depending on which one of us saw it first, we'd often gesture up to the sky at a bald eagle or an osprey. You didn't want to miss seeing one of them. Or it would be a red-tailed hawk passing over with a snake wriggling in its talons. "Got him one," my neighbor would say. It was something to see.

"Never looked for arrowheads down there on the river though," he said. "Mostly I'd be plowing the hayfield up there on the bench, just moving along on the tractor and see an arrowhead sitting there on the dirt and stop and pick it up. Other times I'd see one, but shoot, it was late and I was tired from fighting that old tractor, and I'd just ignore it and plow it under. I never set out to find one. Never thought I had the time, I guess."

He knew I was a poet. I'd even given a talk/reading to a group from the community once. Afterward he told me, "That was real nice, Bob. Never had much interest in poetry myself, but that was real nice."

So I was nervous about it, the looking. But I kept on. I couldn't seem to help myself. I was hungry for arrowheads. They had become something more than mere objects for me. They were blessings; they were mystery. I must have told myself I needed them like I needed poetry, that if I could find one—just one—whole and intact, that I would know the Muse in a whole new way, a more significant way than before. I remember thinking, or hoping at least, that the ancient peoples whose land I traversed would understand my spiritual need.

There are places in the hills around the Clearwater River that are traditional quest sites. Weyakins, they're called, where in centuries past young Nez Perces went to fast and wait for their vision, until they could see a way of knowing and entering the world on their own terms. I wanted a vision of my own. I wasn't interested in ownership or mere possession, but the heart of something, the soul itself. I told myself whatever I needed to, in order to stay another hour along the river, for one more chance to find what I was after. I must have hoped that whatever spirits existed in that place would take pity on me, that they might recognize the honesty of my quest, and unveil a point or a heavy, faceted stone big enough to bring down an elk.

The arrowhead, if only I could find it, was validation. It was contact with the other maker, all makers. It seemed to me that it was about worthiness too. And the patience that earns it.

Over the next three years, I must have gone down the river to hunt for arrowheads no more than five or six times, and I never found anything but chips.

One early spring day after I'd rototilled our garden spot and was raking the soil out in preparation for planting, I spotted an unlikely, shiny stone at the lip of a turned-over clod. It was the bottom half of an arrowhead. No point, but the notches were clear and well made. I was so amazed I called my old arrowhead-hunting friend and accused him of salting my garden spot out of pity. He hadn't. Later that day, I walked down to the neighbor's to show him what I'd found.

"Probably broke the point off with your tiller," he said. "Kinda looks like a fresh break, don't it?" I hadn't wanted to consider that possibility.

After that he took to asking me, almost every time we met, "Find you an arrowhead yet?"

The best time to hunt was just after the river receded from high spring run-off, or in the case of the lower Clearwater, when the Army Corps of Engineers finally closed down the spillway on the dam across the North Fork, upstream at Ahsahka. The river buries and uncovers things continually. After a good runoff, the shore's a completely different place, familiar still but changed too.

So I kept on looking, though not hard. Once or maybe twice a summer I ventured down to the flint fields with a friend or with my wife and kids. Our youngest son, who was eight or nine then, made little distinction between chips and actual arrowheads. Why should he? He'd never even seen someone find a whole arrowhead—and somehow, young as he was, he could happily and patiently hunt and scrape for most of an afternoon without complaint.

It was a hot July day. The sun on its own was brutal, but off the water and rocks it was worse still. We'd get wet in the river to cool off, then go back to our hunting. Just being near the river was enough really. The sound of mountain water is among the most beautiful sounds on earth. Our daughter was upriver a few yards, picking some tart early blackberries. My wife had gotten out a book. Violet, the black Lab, was begging for a thrown stick. And then there it was: an almost perfect arrowhead in my palm. Long one way and narrow the other, a dark, old blood color, there was one extra chunk chipped from the middle, either the maker's mistake or damage sustained in the river's thrash.

I kept looking at it, turning it over and over. I wanted to exclaim but was sure my eyes were deceiving me. I kept thinking I'd turn it over one more time and see that it was all an illusion, that it was just a shard abandoned on the way to an arrowhead. But it was there, almost perfect, and at last I said something.

"I found one."

We passed it around then, and when everyone had looked at and admired it, I put it very carefully in the pocket of my shorts, sat back down on the sand and gravel, and kept on looking. Ten minutes later, I found another.

"Wow," said my son, "you're lucky, Dad," and I agreed that I was, and though I kept on looking another thirty or forty minutes that day, I was done, and a few months after that day we moved away, up into the woods and away from the river, and though I think about the river almost every day and miss the constant old and newness of it, and miss those moments sprawled at its edge, I have not been back to hunt for arrowheads since. I have no need to.

I don't own a thing that belonged to my grandfather, let alone to his father or his father's father. This is understandable, in a way. My grandfather was a coal miner before unions. He never had much of anything to pass on in the first place, though he himself was famous in our family for finding money on the streets—change and paper money both. He must have spent a lot of time looking down, I used to think. It was late in his life. He was walking either to or from the East End Tavern or Blimka's. On good days, he'd find enough money for another beer or two. Two-bits a glass for draught. He had an eye for quarters especially.

I wish I owned something of his. I wonder what happened to his cane, his fedora. Gone. Even something he found along the street—an ancient dollar bill, maybe, a silver certificate. He must have found more than money. Or maybe he let that sort of thing go. Useless, unspendable. He'd put in more than forty years in the mines, finding and digging up and loading what he was sent to find. If it wasn't coal, it wasn't worth finding.

When they showed up at the Clearwater with their backhoes, shake-boxes, and sieves, were those industrial arrowhead hunters looking for treasure, something they might sell? Booty. That seems especially shameful now.

My own children and grandchildren, they'll be luckier. If the three arrowheads currently in my possession get passed on to my kids and their kids, will that matter? *Your great-great grandfather found this along the Clearwater River way back in the 1990's.* And what of the descendants of the people who made them, who may live still on their ancestral lands?

Finding is not the same thing as making.

I think of that student of mine, years ago. How it distressed him that he couldn't "see" what was in a poem on his own. It was only words, a throw of words along a river of syllables.

"The act of reading a poem is no less an important act than the writing of a poem," I said. He regarded me skeptically. That would mean that listening to music was somehow equal to making it, that being undone by the majesty of a great painting would be just as important as having painted it. Was unearthing an arrowhead a critical part in its making?

Yes, I wanted to say. *No,* I thought I should.

That student couldn't see what was in a poem because he had not yet learned to allow himself to see it. He came to the poem with the eyes he brought to every page he had ever read. He approached a page of written language as though it were a hodgepodge of glyphs from which it was his duty to extract some gem of assertion, some useful tidbit of information, a rubble inside of which there must necessarily be an undamaged whole. But what it looked like, in poetry at least, was only more rubble. Familiar-looking rubble, but rubble nonetheless. He could not see from the corner of his eye. He was too busy looking.

It's about seeing. It's always about seeing. On the quest or on the hunt, you believe you will find what it is you seek; you believe it is there, if only you look in the right place, if only you look the right way. And what makes such looking, and therefore the seeing such looking aspires to, difficult, is the sameness of the broken stones, the superfluity of ink or leaves, the camouflage of all that resembles but is not what you seek.

"All right," I said. "You have to learn how to see all over again." I was talking to myself. That's the foundation of teaching; it's trying to see in public, in tandem, there, at ten o'clock from the reddest sumac. The diamonds on the rattlesnake's back are no more than the snubbed-off branch from a ponderosa pine. A point among the tonnage of chips and stones.

I have an old tool chest my father gave me. He bought it just after he was discharged from the navy after World War II. It's made of oak; the drawers are lined with green felt. Its handle is made of an arc of steel and a sewn thong of leather. It's really too beautiful for tools, so I use it for keepsakes. There are special photographs inside, and a silviculturalist's core drill—a tool used by a forester to pull a sample from deep within a tree and gauge by the rings its age or to see if the tree has heart rot (the gift of a friend, it belonged to his father; someday I want to use it just to see, though I haven't yet).

In one of the larger drawers there's the claw of a hawk. I'd come across the carcass on a walk along the river. It had been gnawed on and pretty well scattered, probably by coyotes or bobcats, and there was the talon, a chunk of legbone and some down attached at the top. In a smaller drawer I have arrayed, in a row from largest to smallest, six snake rattles. They came into the yard, those poor snakes, and while they had no concept of property or boundaries, I simply could not allow them to live so near my children. I keep their rattles less as souvenirs than as reminders of my sins and whenever I look at them I still feel a twinge of remorse.

From yet another drawer, I pick out the smallest of three arrowheads. It's half an inch wide, not quite three-quarters of an inch long: a bird point—for a duck or a goose, or a grouse. I can hold it between my thumb and forefinger and almost feel the lives it has touched. There is life and death in it, but more life than death. It is no bauble, no mere decoration, no simple conversation piece. Not for me.

I can see that. The trick is in the saying.

Here's a thing I don't like about Frank Sinatra: the way he called women "broads." Why, given his fondness for the term, did so many women love him anyway? That was then? Then again, the actress Angie Dickinson spoke of being in the thrall of "the stare." He had a way of looking at a woman that made her feel as though the rest of the world had vanished.

Sinatra expected certain things from the world. I have come to believe that he was true to himself, or true at least to the persona he'd fashioned himself into. And who knows if there was really any difference between the two? Asked about jewelry, he replied, "I don't need it. I know who I am." I dislike the presumptive condemnation there, but I like the full-strength certainty. Somehow, this is what Sinatra embodies for me, even now: clear, ringing confidence; a pure and enviable certainty about what matters.

What seems to have mattered most for Sinatra was music, followed by love, friendship, beauty, loyalty, and cool. Everything else could go to hell. According to the musicians he worked with, he was among the most demanding and hard-working artists around. His must have seemed a kind of boorish integrity sometimes; you might not like it, but you had to respect it.

He was "very tough on people," said Nelson Riddle. "If I wasn't conducting to his liking, he shove me out of the way . . . I'd feel awful." I can almost feel sorry for Riddle, but when I listen to the recordings, I can believe that Sinatra was among the best things that ever happened to him.

Then there are the violins. I can hear the artistry in those Riddle, Billy May, or Gordon Jenkins arrangements; I just don't care for what I hear. A lot of it may have had to do with the 1950's, postwar American sense that bigger is better: what the violins were to Sinatra's music, the tail fin was to a Coupe de Ville—a production as big as an asphalt spreader with a waterbed ride. What I love about Sinatra's music lies in the other direction, away from the soporific strings and toward the elements of jazz. He played his voice, which was both unremarkable and unique, the way a great tenor player played the sax. Instrumentalists speak with awe of Sinatra's "phrasing," and they're not talking about the lyrics, though he had that tool as well: the words and their meanings, the implied narrative, the emotional intensity of meaning, as well as the player's deployment of musical notes.

I idolized Sinatra when I was a boy coming of age, or coming to the awareness that I would inevitably have to be something called "a man." My mother tells me the whole family saw *From Here to Eternity* in the mid-fifties, as a second feature at the Sky-Vue Drive-In. I would have been in the back seat and probably asleep, no more than five or six at the time. Maybe something from that film has stayed with me—not just Sinatra but the whole aura of big-screen heroes of the time. I swear I've seen hundreds of movies about World War II (they were my father's favorites), and as I look back at the men who fought and acted, I'm not sure whether it was art imitating life or the other way around. To this day, I've never seen *The Man With the Golden Arm* or *The Manchurian Candidate*, said to be Sinatra's finest roles, but then movies are not the source of my memories of him. Somehow Sinatra's voice is in me deeper than his image, deeper than memory, maybe. I suspect that I heard him singing while I was still in the womb, maybe the Axel Stordahl arrangement of "Body and Soul," with its transcendent Bobby Hackett trumpet solo, or something earlier still—like "I'll Never Smile Again," which Sinatra recorded in 1940 with Tommy Dorsey. There's a heavy 78 of that one I imagine packed away somewhere in my parents' basement. I knew there were other singers in the world. Singing happened in church, after all, and my father was periodically fixated on great opera tenors too—Caruso, Bjorling, and so on. But the more I try to sift back through things the more convinced I am that, for a while at least, I made no distinction between the verb *to sing* and the name Sinatra.

I no longer idolize Frank Sinatra the man (I'm too old to idolize anybody), and though I even dislike certain things about him, I will always love his art. At least, I've come to that. To use Cole Porter's words, it's "so deep in my heart that [it's] really a part of me." It feels genetic. Sinatra is "under my skin," bone deep, and the difficulty I have had in gaining a measure of intellectual and emotional distance on him is connected directly to his powerful presence in my life, a presence that goes well beyond the voice wafting from the speakers. However, the voice is still what takes me back to a time when the world I lived in seemed, if only seemed, above all else safe.

I'm eleven, cross-legged on the floor in front of my parents' space-age hi-fi. My father sits in his designated easy chair and snaps his fingers or taps his foot, and I study the album's cover, the photograph of a thin-haired, lean crooner they call "The Voice." It's May or June, not miserably hot and humid yet in the southern Illinois suburbs of St. Louis, so the windows are open and you can hear the birds going at it outside, if you listen past the music. Less than two hundred miles south the white civic leaders of Memphis are worried about the "threat" of integration. It will be a couple of years yet until the 1964 Civil Rights Act is passed into law, and a few more after that until the Gulf of Tonkin incident, which will be used to justify sending ground troops to Vietnam. (US military advisors are already there.) Stan Musial is playing his second-to-last season as a St. Louis Cardinal. In a few months, some kids my age will begin having what psychologists will call "nuclear nightmares," in response to the Cuban missile crisis. But none of this matters to me yet, and none of it matters to my father. We're living in a brief period of calm, and inside that period is an even shorter one of sweet equilibrium and contentment that will last only as long as it takes one side of a 33 to play or for my mother to slice the meatloaf, mash the spuds, or heat up a can of peas. During this tiny interlude, a nightly occurrence, everything is as it should be, or at least it feels that way. But I must have been aware that things were happening out in the world, and something was happening to me as well.

I must have felt it there, even if I couldn't have said what it was. Maybe I was just learning about life, or perhaps about the sublime, how it was something one human being was capable of making another feel. I understood that when Sinatra urged us all to "drink up" and to "order anything you see," the impulse behind his generosity was in fact a pain that nothing could make any better, except maybe the singing itself. Whoever "Angel Eyes" might have been, the loss of her was somehow both insurmountable and the occasion for the most exquisite kind of saying. "'Scuse me," the last line goes, "while I disappear." Here was a man dealing with a broken heart; this was how it was done. Sinatra was emblematic of the era, both my childhood and my father's young manhood. He was a very sensitive kind of steel, a resilient and powerful dreamer, and he became for me a true American icon, a personal paradigm, a man the likes of whom I could, for better or worse, aim to be.

Those caricatures of the young Sinatra, so skinny he disappears behind the microphone stand, are part of the connection too. I was an extremely skinny kid, for one thing, and there are family photographs, roughly the same vintage as the cartoons of Sinatra, in which my father seems to be the person for whom the phrase "painfully thin" was coined. Also my father was handsome in his own way. Not extravagantly handsome, not pretty. In fact, he was like Sinatra: handsome enough and, more important, of a bearing, with a set of the jaw and the blue eyes and the devil-may-care gesture to make it all seem like more than it was. I'm sure my father must have styled himself after Sinatra, but by the time I was most deeply under the spell of The

Voice, it was no longer my father but his younger brother, Uncle Bob, my namesake, who was for me Sinatra's correlative. My father was a working man, a long-time civilian employee for the Air Force, and he wore a workingman's clothes and fell asleep at the end of a long day on the job in the same easy chair he would sit in later, after dinner, listening to records before leaving for his night job selling cars. His mouth lolled open; the newspaper drifted down from his lap onto the floor. He did not look like someone destined to be called "the Chairman of the Board."

On the other hand, Uncle Bob was a white-collar cop, a small-town police commissioner and constable, and the head of security over the river at Stix, Baer, and Fuller, one of St. Louis's largest department stores. Unlike my father, he wore tailored suits and narrow ties, Sinatra's kind of canted hat. And even when he wasn't in his work clothes, he looked as though he was dressed for golf or "cocktails," whatever those were: slacks creased sharp enough to slice paper, brilliantly shined shoes, and a gold, monogrammed ring the size of a walnut on his finger. I'm told he had a fine voice and often sang at weddings, but I don't remember ever hearing him sing. My sister and I stopped by his house one afternoon, and there was his pal Pat and, of all people, Frankie Avalon. They'd just finished a round of golf and were sitting around the dining room table, drinking something clear in tall, frosted glasses. Frankie Avalon looked like what he was, a pretty boy. Uncle Bob, on the other hand, looked the way he always did: seriously at ease, very cool, eminently powerful.

Uncle Bob seemed to live in several worlds at once. It wasn't only that you might run into somebody like Frankie Avalon at his house; he was always connecting with significant people. He brought an inscribed Eddy Arnold album home to his daughter for her birthday once, and another time he stopped by our house to hand me a three-by-five note card with the autographs of Roger McGuinn, Gene Clark, and David Crosby on it—half of the Byrds. When I asked how he managed such a thing, he just winked. And once, rubbernecking in the foyer of a fancy downtown St. Louis restaurant with my prom date, I spotted him in one of the dozens of celebrity photographs arrayed across the walls. He was posed smiling alongside a famous actor of the day, and it pleases me now that I can't remember who—Tony Curtis, Gregory Peck . . . it could have been anyone.

Like my father, Uncle Bob was the son of a coal miner; like my father he grew up impoverished in the midst of the Depression. He was part of the same family as the rest of us, yet he seemed noble somehow, a kind of charming and beloved royal rogue. My grandmother loved telling us stories of the women he dated in his youth. They were always "beautiful girls" or "real lookers," and invariably they were "crazy about Bob." I knew instinctively that this was true. More than once we had run into him at work while we shopped downtown, and he'd walk the department store floors with us for a while, flirting with the salesgirls and elevator operators. He gaze seemed a gift to them. His easy banter was Cary Grant suave. And if there was anything in the reactions of those women to my uncle less than outright movie star idolatry, I couldn't see it. It's still said, a bittersweet testimonial in our family mythology, that when people saw him coming, they beamed.

And under his left shoulder, in a snap-draw, tooled leather holster, hung a chrome Smith & Wesson snub-nosed .38. There were things he knew about, things we likely couldn't even imagine. Family legend has it that he had once dated the daughter of Buster Wortman, a former Capone lieutenant who'd fled south when the Chicago mob disintegrated. Wortman had set up shop in St. Louis but lived across the river in less populated and more laissez-faire southern Illinois. His house, just a few miles outside my hometown, was angular and "ultramodern," surrounded by a moat stocked with bluegill. I used to ride my bike out there to fish now and then, and I can't imagine how it is I even knew about the place, unless Uncle Bob had taken me there before. It was Uncle Bob who taught me to fish, just as it was he who first put a gun in my hands when I was thirteen. On a gray, cloudy day—late fall or early spring?—the clout of my heart almost obscured his whispered instructions at my ear. Then the great blast: the target was a gallon cider jug afloat in a pond, and on the second shot—me ten paces closer, ears still ringing—it shattered and vanished.

"Bingo," Uncle Bob said, easing the rifle from my hands. "Nice shot." I had never felt such a fantastic, body-tingling zing. Seven years later I would be both a GI and a conscientious objector, refusing to take up arms at all.

FFI can recall just two pieces of advice Uncle Bob gave me. The first, regarding the draft then looming just over a year in my future, was this: "Whatever you do, don't volunteer. Never volunteer." He'd been a marine, but at the best possible time, between the end of World War II and the deadly preview of coming attractions called the "conflict" in Korea. The second suggestion had to do with grooming. He pushed his Oleg Cassini hat back on his head, cupped my chin in his hand, surveyed the darkening fuzz I'd brought along by way of a mustache, then said, "Bobby, never cultivate anything on your face that grows wild on your ass." I'd wonder later what his advice might have been if he could have seen me a few years later, my hair to my shoulders, an American flag sewn to the back pocket of my jeans.

Once when my father and I tagged along with him on some ordinary errand, I heard Uncle Bob describe a threat he'd made to some small-time, smart-ass St. Louis hood who'd caused trouble in the store. I wish I could remember what he said. All that comes back to me is the quick tickle inside, a little silent whoop of luscious fear, although it might have been no more than a dip in the road we drove. We were moving toward the deep dark end of the sixties. The world was treacherous, but as long as Uncle Bob was around, we seemed invulnerable. We were our own Rat Pack. There was nothing we couldn't handle. And we were happy.

When Uncle Bob died of a heart attack, at forty-two, in 1969, the year I graduated from high school, I was devastated and enraged. I refused from that moment on to consider the existence of a God, although I was nevertheless willing to blame Him not only for my uncle's death but also for the dreadful state of our nation, by then twisted by assassinations and free-falling into a war in which young men I knew were dying, and over which my father and I would nearly come to despise one another.

On the day of Uncle Bob's burial, the line of mourners' cars stretched for a mile across town, from the undertaker's nearly to the cemetery. The notice box on the funeral home's front lawn said "Robert Wrigley Funeral." We were in a white stretch limo: my grandparents, Uncle Bob's wife and daughter, my father, mother, sister and me. It was a sunny day in June. The town was awash in blossoms, but everything looked dead and dying to me. The mid-day headlights of mourners' cars receded out of sight behind us; I counted fifty and then looked over at my father, who studied his hands folded on his knees. We were at the brink of something, he and I and the country as well. There was a new and frightening world out there, without the sense of optimism and possibility, without the slick swing and polish Sinatra so exemplified—even if it was an illusion. Just then it seemed that the man we were about to bury had been all that stood between us and our own impending doom.

There's a photograph of Sinatra leading Jacqueline Kennedy, storybook ravishing in her inaugural gown, up a flight of stairs toward the action. Sinatra had produced the show, and in the picture he's gallant, a step above her and turning back, plainly solicitous but wide-eyed and wary as well, as though he knows he's been entrusted with a goddess even loftier than his beloved and lost Ava Gardner. In another photo from that evening, Sinatra and JFK are laughing together. Really laughing. The new president has a cigar in his left hand, Sinatra's got the usual Chesterfield. I wish I knew what was so funny. The scene can't be, but it looks . . . *innocent*. You can almost believe the complete rightness of the night and the still-open, honest possibilities for the nation.

Out of that decade would come what are now the old stories. JFK's brains blown out, the country ripped apart by an illegal war, a civil rights struggle that revealed a festering lie inside the Constitution. About this time, Sinatra's rumored ties to the Mafia became a topic of conversation: Frank Sinatra, whose stage-managed gala had ushered in the reign of beauty, grace, and love into the White House. How it all must have galled him. How it must have embittered him. He blamed Bobby Kennedy, who, as attorney general and senator, had taken on organized crime relentlessly. Then next thing we all knew Sinatra was switching political affiliations, and I hate this part especially: the way Sinatra's cool and the killer grin turned nasty; the way, in five short and murderous years, the Duke of Camelot was transformed into the Dark Frog Prince of San Clemente. Richard Nixon, for godsakes—the antithesis of suave, the Snopes King triumphant. How far we had fallen, and how fast.

Then began the long and never-ending exodus of high-profile Democrats to the Republican party, in my working-class family the approximate moral equivalent of handing the man the nails as he crucified Jesus. There was Augie Busch, the Budweiser mogul who owned my beloved St. Louis Cardinals. (It was late in the eighties before I became a fan again.) I don't remember the others; they were legion. "Democrats for Nixon," they called themselves. I don't care about them. But I remember Sinatra. His embrace of Nixonian politics was something I took personally, facing as I was the relatively imminent prospect of my own induction into the army and the genuine possibility of Vietnam. That dashing arrogance I had once wanted to emulate, that stare I'd still like to accomplish—it all repulsed me. My rage was intense, and I made myself believe my disgust included his music, the music of my father and my uncle and millions of people like them, who sat in front of their stereos and listened on, blind to the ruin accruing all around them, deaf to truer and more terrifying music rising up from their children.

In the year and a half between the death of his brother and my being drafted into the army, my father became a sullen, worrisome presence in the household, while I was an angry young man, my hair grown long, as I sported—Uncle Bob's advice notwithstanding—an insufficient mustache. I hung posters of Abbie Hoffman and Malcolm X in my room, taped an upside-down American flag in the window, and quit going to my college classes. Next to Jimi Hendrix, the Rolling Stones, and Janis Joplin, Sinatra was a lackey of the elite, a mouthpiece for oppressive conformity. His music was no more than a distraction, decorative, full of ludicrous romantic pap and unwilling to confront the rot at the heart of our American world. If you had asked me then, I would have told you that Sinatra's music was little better than Lawrence Welk's.

According to some sort of accepted wisdom, or the traditional code, when the nation called, its young people would respond. The story still goes the same way: it's about freedom and responsibility—the freedom others like ourselves had fought for and died to preserve; the responsibility of all subsequent generations to carry on. Anything less, anything else at all, is dishonor. I tried to believe it, but I could not. I think I nearly came to envy my father and his generation.

My father also found himself overwhelmed by the national dilemma. He was a veteran of the navy in World War II, and by the late sixties he'd worked for the military another two decades and more. The present and its war were nothing like the past, but what other model was there? If there was no leaving America, there was no thoughtless loving it either. Not for me. By 1970, in the face of growing public opposition and congressional cutbacks, the military was feeding on its own muscle to keep the war going. The long hair, the peace symbol on the back bumper of my car, even the books I was reading—*The Autobiography of Malcolm X*, Abbie Hoffman's *Revolution for the Hell of It*—must have seemed an affront to my father. I've written poems about those days, mostly highly stylized pieces, all fraught with rhymes, little distancing mechanisms I needed to get the story down. Even now, three decades later, it's hard to write about such things in the unblinking cadences of prose. The fact is, I baited my father. I said things about the nation out of anger and fear, but I think I also wanted to see how hard I might push him away from what he claimed to believe, and in the process away from me. We pounded the table and shook our fists, even as the numbers rolled up: the weekly dead, the armadas of planes disgorging their cargoes of flag-draped caskets.

I no longer take much pride in the fact that this was an argument I would eventually win. Time has confirmed, to me at least, the historical accuracy of my positions, even as the years have made me feel ashamed at how I treated my father. Most often the battles occurred at the dinner table, which was really the only place we saw one another regularly: my mother believed in the daily breaking of bread, the gathering that symbolically at least might sustain or even heal us as a family. But something would start us off—Walter Cronkite's weekly recitation of the body count usually—and we'd be off. At the end of one of our worst arguments, my father, red-faced and sputtering, set his fork clattering in his dinner plate.

"If there was an easy way out of this goddamned war, don't you think they'd take it?" he said.

My mother and sister, veterans of the home-front war that raged each night, sat silent and waited for what came next. The TV blathered on.

"Just stop," I said, and then I started to laugh. "If I go over there and die, what are you gonna tell people I died for? To keep California safe from communism?"

"We've got to stop them somewhere . . . ." But he wasn't lecturing anymore. He'd heard all this before; we both heard all the arguments repeatedly. But this time I had laughed, and the laugh said that he was not just wrong, but foolish. "Goddammit, it's a lot more complicated than you think, Bob." Another old standby line.

"Go ahead and explain it to me then." I leaned back and twiddled my thumbs, smug. "I'm listening."

"The people who got us into this war aren't stupid—"

"No," I said, "they're not. They're worse than stupid, they're evil."

"Shut up!" He jumped up and rocked the table. My sister caught her wobbling glass of milk. "Just shut the hell up! I don't want to hear this. I'm so goddamned sick of this." He was walking away from the table toward the living room. "I'm just so sick of this."

"Someday you'll see," I said, and someday he did. Only now I hate my gloating tone of voice, the sanctimoniousness. Nor can I forget the sadness I felt then, as I watched his resolve begin to crumble.

My father believed that there was nothing his generation of Americans could not accomplish, and I almost envy him such straightforward optimism. What they didn't know, they would figure out, and what they knew, they knew best. It seems to me that Sinatra's arrogance was archetypically mid-twentieth century, new Americanism, just as his excesses were. The country and the crooner could both be thuggish, and all too often; the glamorous overdoing of things bespeaks the violins as well as the dams, poisoned rivers, clear-cuts, and other disasters of post-war capitalist techno-euphoria.

For my father, like almost everyone else, the sixties was a pageant of premature deaths that began with the assassination of JFK and ended (well, the decade did) with the death of his brother. It's a monstrous list and everybody knows it, from the Kennedys and Martin Luther King, Jr., through Malcolm X, Medgar Evers, the tens of thousands of names now on the Wall in Washington, DC, not to mention the innumerable lost Vietnamese. None of those deaths seemed heroic;

rather, we were moving martyr by martyr toward chaos. Death was contagious and coming closer and when, in 1970, my draft lottery number came up 66, you could almost feel it at the windows looking in. I felt like I had a guaranteed ticket to Vietnam.

In the months before I was drafted, I went several times to St. John's Cemetery. I sat next to Uncle Bob's headstone and talked not so much to him as to someone with my own name who might know more than I did. I could see my face in the polished granite.

"What should I do?" I asked. "What is the right thing?" I thought about the Marines' Hymn, played at Uncle Bob's funeral. *Semper fidelis*, the marines' motto went—"always faithful." To the Corps, to the country, to honor and duty. Where did my world fit in? Where did I?

"I need to know," I said, and I remember waiting a long time, on several occasions, for an answer, for a sign. In the afternoon, a silver maple cast its shade over the grave, and from that spot in the cemetery I could look from the bluffs out over the flood-plain flats to St. Louis. The belts of smog from the steel mills, foundries, and chemical plants turned the sunsets bloody. When I was a boy, I used to ride my bike through the cemetery to get to this spot. I thought the crimson light was beautiful. I felt as if I were on a mountain. Among my buried kin, I waited.

In October 1970, I applied to my local draft board for reclassification from 1A to 1A-O, which would make me officially a conscientious objector but one who was willing to be drafted, "available for noncombatant duty only." It was a half-hearted attempt. I couldn't bring myself to apply for full conscientious objector status. A straight 1-O classification would have kept me from being drafted at all; I'd have been obligated to serve two years of alternative service, in a VA hospital or some other public facility. But to have done so would have been to renege completely on the code my father at least still believed in. In my application to the draft board, I explained that I was willing to serve in the military, that my father and uncle had both been veterans, but that my beliefs in nonviolence made it impossible for me to serve as a regular foot soldier.

My application was approved in early December. My draft notice arrived on my twentieth birthday, February 27, 1971. What I did not know was that the army's policy for dealing with CO's, most of them claiming religious grounds for their classifications, was to make them all medics. So much for noncombatant duty. I would learn very shortly that my military occupational specialty—my MOS—would be, by the army's coded system, "91-Bravo-10." Or, in plain English, "combat medical corpsman." The only difference between me and all the other foot soldiers in Vietnam would be that I would not have been given any rifle or weapons training whatsoever. I would learn this and a lot more.

The day I reported for induction, March 12, 1971, my mother and father and girlfriend took me to the county courthouse to board the bus to St. Louis for processing. There were quite a few of us waiting in the lobby, young men and their families from the towns nearby. I knew a few of them. When it was time to leave, I hugged my folks each in turn, but it was my father's embrace that lasted longest. I tried to pull myself away, but he wouldn't let go.

"I'll be OK, Dad," I said. I didn't know if I believed it or not. He was still holding me tight. Other men were climbing onto the bus.

"Just come back," he said into the air behind my ear. "I just need you to come back."

He kept his eyes down as I kissed my girlfriend once more. I remember I winked at her and probably grinned—a leftover Sinatra riff.

"Play it cool," my father said, and I got on the bus.

I don't know when I noticed his white car following behind. Ten or twelve miles of two-lane state highway and he made no move to pass. I tried not to look back, but when the bus hit the four-lane interchange, I turned fully around. We sped down the ramp onto the interstate toward St. Louis, and I watched as my father's car kept going straight, down Highway 159 into the north end of town, toward home.

That night, at Fort Leonard Wood in central Missouri, we got off the bus and, in order that we might be recognizable as trainees in our civilian clothes, were issued old, recycled fatigue jackets. After checking my paperwork, one of the Spec 4's behind the counter shouted out, "Hey, we got us a CO here!" and for a moment or two I was the center of a peculiar attention in the room. The field jacket they gave me was ragged and stained.

"That's blood, trainee," the Spec 4 said. I'm sure it wasn't. I remember thinking that I was hungry. "You might as well get used to it. All you CO's get to be medics, and after the radio operator, the doc's Charlie's favorite target."

They were laughing behind the counter, but I kept my face as blank as the wind. I don't blame them for laughing really. I was not sure that they didn't know me better than I knew myself.

Two days later I was shipped out to Fort Sam Houston, in San Antonio, Texas, home of the US Army Medical Training center, where I wound up a trainee in Echo-4, a company made up entirely of CO's, probably three-hundred men in all. We were every race and ethnic background; most of the men were there because of religious beliefs. On any given night there would be serious Bible study and spit-shining going on at one end of the barracks, while at the other end there convened an impromptu roundtable on the sweet seductions of the era's most available psychedelic drugs—and in the middle a lecture on the multifariousness of sexual raptures. I met a man whose name I can no longer remember, who loved poetry and could recite Edwin Muir's "The Horses" from memory. I met a man named Skip, a Seventh-Day Adventist whose most passionate hope was that, instead of going to Vietnam, he'd get orders to join the "Whitecoats," who were all stationed near Washington, DC, and who would be the subjects of the military's experiments with various combat-likely diseases and their treatments. I met Grimes, from Hoboken, New Jersey, who had a speed habit and played a bluesy stride piano Saturday nights in the day room. And I met Devereaux, from Minnesota, who told me the third week of our basic training that he intended to apply for reclassification to full 1-O status and discharge.

"Can you do that?"

"Yes," he said. "I've talked on the phone to the counseling people. They've got an office in San Antonio, and I'm going there as soon as we get a pass." And he did, a few weeks later, and I went with him.

The American Friends Service Committee had a storefront in downtown San Antonio. It's a Quaker organization, though the only proselytizing that went on had to do with the war and the Selective Service System. I spoke to the counselor there just once, and though I remember what he said—the way it had to work, the army's requisite hoops and hot coals—I can't bring back his face or his voice. The session took thirty minutes or so. When we left, we walked down the block and visited the Alamo.

In June I applied for discharge, claiming that since my induction I had had a change of heart, that knowing what I knew now I was certain that I would not be able to faithfully serve, not even in a noncombatant role. To make such an application turned you into a military *persona non grata*, even as it passed you through a revolving door into a kind of command-administrative limbo. On the day of my company's "graduation" from medical training, about thirty percent of us received orders for Vietnam. I was one of those, but my application for discharge kept me instead—at least temporarily—at Fort Sam, part of a misfit company called STD, or Special Training Detachment. We were mostly CO's, with a couple of gays, and others referred to simply as "212's," men deemed "unfit for military service": a pair of bedwetters, one robust and muscular man who had punched out three sergeants so far, and a variety of other oddballs and straight-out crazies.

All those last endless five months in the army, the music in the barracks was Jethro Tull, Derek and the Dominoes, Sly and the Family Stone, Jefferson Airplane. One night a strange, wonderful saxophone music floated softly over the bunks—a ballad, but not like anything I'd ever heard before. It was almost three-dimensional, like a human being walking among us as music. It had a body. I got up from my bunk and headed toward it. The tape belonged to Armstrong, one of the old guys among us, twenty-four, Black and prematurely balding, a wiry, even frail-looking guy who every Sunday morning preached the gospel emphatically across an on-end footlocker.

"Who's that playing?" I asked.

"That," he said, "is Lester Young. He an angel."

The little, one-speaker portable cassette player's tinniness didn't obscure the lush beauty of Young's playing. I was, I think, remembering something I didn't know I knew, nor did I know that Lester Young had been dead for more than a decade that first time I heard him play.

There's a story, which may be apochryphal, about Young's last days. He spent all day, every day, the story went, listening obsessively to the phrasings and riffs not of another horn player but of Frank Sinatra. Not even my father listened to Sinatra in those days, though I don't know why. Maybe all that "swinging" seemed frivolous in the face of the weekly slaughter. Somehow a lover's broken heart had been devalued in the light of a mother's grief, or a widow's, or a child's.

I learned to be a combat medic but never was one. I met people who might have been Quakers. I wrote an application for discharge in which I laid out my philosophy as a pacifist in any and every situation, though I never truly was one. I was guided by the Friends to the writings and teachings of Henry David Thoreau, Martin Luther King, Jr., and Gandhi. I learned about the long tradition of conscientious objection, and I wondered: had it been thirty years before, during World War II, would I have had the nerve to do what I was doing? Would I have believed then what I was claiming to believe now?

While I was in the army things were changing for my father

51

too. He was learning to live with his own revised expectations, his diminished faith, a sad measure of political and patriotic relativism. In November I was honorably discharged. I had vowed that I would not accept anything less. I hadn't done anything wrong; I'd abided by all the rules, such as they were. But that's probably not true. By the time I was discharged, I probably would have accepted any way out the army might have offered me.

When I arrived home, determined to ride my abbreviated GI Bill benefits as far as I could toward a college degree, I found my father happy as hell to see me, though I noticed too that his satisfaction at my safe return did not bring back his old playfulness or his once unflappable sense of certainty. Somehow he seemed bereft, a little bit lost, feeling his way carefully for words and struggling now to understand what was right or wrong about the nation's situation, or why.

Compared to the seeming glory and righteous sacrifice of World War II, my father's war, Vietnam looked small and hideous, although the stench of it fouled the air far out of proportion to its size. Not only was there no happy end, there was no end at all. There may never be. And over the years I have come to wonder if, in some ways, my father's generation suffered almost as much from the effects of the Vietnam war as mine did. Maybe the litany of public murders in the sixties cauterized my patriotic wound just as Uncle Bob's death sealed me off from religious belief. All I know is that by the time I was drafted I believed that I had few illusions about the men (they were always men, of course) in charge of the nation's collective fate. My father, on the other hand, had to suffer each national calamity, each lie, each blunder—all of it—like a corrosive poured weekly into his blood. In the end, much of what he believed about the country his generation had helped build to world prominence was shaken, weakened, even destroyed. In a way, his heart was broken.

I thought I knew about heartbreak somehow, though at the

time I believed myself immune to it. My mother has told me that sometimes my father could not sleep during those nights. He would get up and go downstairs and listen to music turned low. It might have been a kind of refuge for him. I don't know what he listened to; my mother left him alone there. Maybe it was Sinatra, and if it was, I imagine it was the mournful ballads of loneliness and loss he favored. Sad catharsis, those tunes about love gone wrong—in my father's case, maybe the love of the land. He was one of the walking wounded then. He looked it, for a while.

And yet, by some miracle, come 1972 we found ourselves, my father and I, working together for the election of that good harbinger of Democratic moral superiority and ruin, George McGovern. At the same time, as a cost-cutting move, the Defense Department offered early retirement to a few thousand of its civilian employees in every branch of the services, including the air force, and my father took them up on it. He was only fifty, but the previous years had cost him. All the while that we were blundering into Vietnam, my father had spent his days among the necessarily duty-bound, the military troops who believed in the traditional code, and he loved and admired them. He spent his nights at home with his family, with me, in another world entirely, where he and I had been at war—or, rather, where I had been at war with the nation and he was its nervous, uncertain representative.

"You were right all along," he said to me, when I came home from the army. It was not a grudging concession, but it wasn't a happy one either. He sounded now and then the way he did when his brother died. That was when I felt again that other sort of shame, as though it had been I and not history that had killed in my father some myth he loved.

Sinatra was absent from my life for a long time, all through college and at least a decade beyond. I was reinventing myself in a new place—Montana, where I was tutored by, among others, the great

American poet and World War II bombardier Richard Hugo, and where I took somewhat to his brand of mid-century swing music. I also tried early on to like country music—there was not a lot in the way of alternatives on the 1970's airwaves of the American West—but it didn't take. Eventually, I gave myself over to that vague familiar, the poultice of jazz, the supreme American artistic achievement, and I was swept away.

Jazz was new and old for me at the same time. I remembered that down at the other, somewhat less busy end of his record cabinet, my father also favored music by Dave Brubeck, Nat King Cole, Sarah Vaughn, and Lionel Hampton. Soon, on my own, I discovered Sidney Bechet, Bud Powell, Charles Mingus, and John Coltrane. I was in love all of a sudden with a music that came, tellingly, from a generation or more before my own, and I was falling inside rhythms that spoke volumes without lyrics. Jazz was about heartbreak and joy; it was exuberant and mournful; it was eloquently clear. But more than that, jazz came openly and honestly from the fallen world, a place full of darknesses that were real and political as well as personal. Jazz hid nothing, whitewashed nothing. It rose up from the horrors of slavery and racism and strode forth triumphant and transcendent. At first I resisted lyrics entirely—I didn't want the music muddied up with additional meaning—but when I made my way among the great singers of jazz, I came to Billie Holiday, to Johnny Hartman; the way their lyrics could hang and flow over a melody was like silk, and I found myself back where I'd started, listening as a child. Ella Fitzgerald, for instance, was one of my father's favorites too.

In 1990, when I visited the Midwest to see my parents, my father took me to his favorite used record store in St. Louis. It was a little city of vinyl and a motherlode of jazz. There was everything, and I blew a lot more money than I could afford: Coltrane's *Black Pearls*; some Dexter Gordon, Paul Desmond, and Ahmad Jamal; Bill Evans, Coleman Hawkins, Helen Humes; and what at the time seemed like a concession to my father, to the bond that music had been between us years before—a pair of records by Sinatra. One was a 1967 studio session called *Francis A. & Edward K.* a terrific collaboration between Sinatra and Duke Ellington and his band. The other was a double Capitol reissue: twenty chestnuts arranged by Gordon Jenkins, tight and impeccable, and, yes, flamboyant with strings. In the few days of my visit we had left, my father and I probably played those Sinatra records half a dozen times or more. The weeping violins bothered me—they always will—but no one ever made me believe the lyrics to "Mood Indigo" before; no one else had ever made the sweet lie of Hoagy Carmichael's "I Get Along Without You Very Well" break my heart.

Even then I would have said my reintroduction to Sinatra was more a nod to my father than my own fall back under the singer's spirit. Plainly my father was glad that we were together, and just as plainly he was glad that his music could make my heart glad too. We sat and listened at the same dining room table we had argued over years before. Sinatra was singing "Last Night When We Were Young." Everything seemed almost simple again. Everything seemed to be forgiven. "Ages ago, last night." Maybe it was only the front edge of that inevitable nearing-in-time all children and parents experience: when I was one year old, my father was thirty times my age; now I've lived almost two-thirds as many years as he has. Our lives, once unimaginable to each other, looked clearer at last. "Life was a star," Sinatra sang, "a song unsung." Perhaps during that visit it was simply that we began to pick up the threads, like a melody.

With Sinatra's music came a kind of grace, and I mean that in the spiritual sense. In the first place, it is extraordinary music. If the great Lester Young was obsessed with Sinatra at the end, it was for a good reason. There's little in American popular music as good as Sinatra singing Cole Porter's "Under My Skin." The music also offered me a time-capsule glimpse of my father's young manhood, when he was the age I had been when I asked my dead uncle's tombstone what to do. How similar were we, I wonder? And how could we have been so different? As young men, we both believed in our respective ways of understanding the world. We were both naïve, I'm sure. But I envy him his illusions, if that's what they were. I hear them in Sinatra's "Too Marvelous for Words"—its sweet, exuberant joy. What a marvelous thing, to be so in love with a someone, with a vision, with a country, with the everything tomorrow might bring.

I'm at home now, in Idaho, and I've got Sinatra going on the stereo. Among the mawkish violins, the tacky grandeur he sometimes favored, Sinatra breathes—you can hear him. Now he's properly mourned and celebrated, and thanks to the humdrum wonders of contemporary recording technology (in this case, a remastered LP digitized on a compact disk), I can sit and listen to him pull that ordinary, if nicotine blue, forty-year-old air inside him, then change it into glory. I'm old enough at last to claim my love for Sinatra, even the lavish, corny splendor of so many of his impeccably overproduced recordings.

The CD is on its second time around, "Three Coins in the Fountain" is on again. It's a movie tune, and now and then the strings burst forth as incongruously as a boutonniere on a butcher's apron. But that's Sinatra, vividly and abundantly Sinatra, and during the regular verses his voice is soft, even vulnerable, and you really can hear him breathe. It's beautiful. The next tune, "What Is This Thing Called Love," gets the same treatment, but there's a wailing Gershwinian clarinet counterpointing the voice, and the mood, from the moment Sinatra enters the song, is deeply and profoundly indigo.

My first decade, the fifties, were numbingly conformist and paranoid. If you happened to have skin that was not white, they were much worse. I understand this. What I want to understand is my own childhood, the comfortable, reassuring illusions of it. Not the patriotic simplicity and jingoism. I mean, rather, the sense that everything was cool, or soon would be. By now the attitude is purely personal; it's all about my models for manhood—none of them perfect, I admit, but I love them all. I love the way they took care of me and showed me things and made me laugh; I love the way they seemed strong, even invincible, and I love, I really love, the music they gave me.

I'm six or seven. My father's left arm and my Uncle Bob's right arm—young, strong, and muscular—are draped out the car's windows. Sinatra snaps his fingers as he sings—I can hear it—and all I can see is the gleaming dash, and their legs, and a little of the road in front of us. They've let me sit up front between them, even though I've got on short pants. We pass down Main Street, and they admire the reflection of the Mercury in the store windows. On the radio, Sinatra sings "All the Way." Whatever that might mean I cannot imagine, but I am along for the ride, happy to be between two men I adore, whose solid presence comforts and instructs me.

Now I've come all the way back to the music. I play Sinatra for my own children. They don't know what to do with it yet, and I don't know how to explain it. I tell them, "Just listen to the words," and they do, for a while. But then they're off after their own lives. My daughter, who is eleven, loves the Beatles. Some mornings on the way to the school bus, she'll be listening to them on her headphones and singing along "all you need is love, love, love is all you need."

I haven't said enough about passion, the kind Sinatra sang about: the silly, funny, crazy, doomed, punishing, and beautiful religion of heartache and romance. Where else could I have learned it? I believe it was implanted in me, that little kid so many years ago squatted in front of the hi-fi speaker. I was hearing how a woman could be "under my skin" and, oh my, even then I couldn't wait. I believed in "this

57

thing called love" long before I felt it, and maybe believing is all there is. My children see me making dinner some nights, singing along, dropping to one knee and clowning for my wife, and I think they do understand, maybe. They will someday, I hope. I believe Sinatra taught me how to fall in love. At least he taught me what it feels like to be someone in the heart of it and not afraid to say so. And he was not wrong. If I had the snapshots, I'd show you now: that's me on the floor, gaptoothed and amazed, grinning up at my parents, who have all of a sudden begun a murmurous slow dance in the middle of the living room. Or make it a home movie—that wink I once saw Uncle Bob give his wife across the dining room table, and the way she blushed then and looked down, smiling.

Over the years I've wondered which one of this trinity of men was the truest source of my carriage and my dreams. My hunches shift and rearrange themselves. I study the old photographs and see that my father truly did resemble Sinatra; I think about the past and realize that my uncle behaved like him. I would insult my father not to make him preeminent, he who gave me Sinatra in the first place, and in some ways I will always see Uncle Bob in the stopped time of arrested motion, a kind of snapshot portrait that places him in an imprecise otherworld between the dailiness of my father and the rarefied air of the great singer at the height of his powers. And yet I cannot separate them; I just can't. The year is 1999. Sinatra's dead at eighty-two, my father is seventy-seven, my uncle's been dead for thirty years but lives in his prime in my memory, like a recording from that same seemingly placid era when Sinatra sang his best.

On the walls of my writing studio, on the desks and shelves, and on the windowsills, I have arrayed certain artifacts by which I have come to know myself. My uncle Bob's shining silver badge with my name on it, pinned to the wall. Here's my discharge orders framed, with "Reason: Conscientious Objection" highlighted. Sinatra peers off a CD jacket at me. And in this picture, my father's dressed in a snazzy sport coat. He's got his leg up on the bumper of his slick '46 Chevy, his right fist at his belt to hold the coat back. His smile is as big as it gets. Sinatra says he's got the world on a string. How could it not be true?

OF FAILURE AND SHADOWS

In early 1987, Robert Penn Warren was named the first "Poet Laureate of the United States." There wasn't that much about it in the papers. Apparently, Senator Spark Matsunaga, a Democrat from Hawaii and a "lover of poetry," had been pushing for such an appointment for a long time, and he found in Daniel Boorstin, then the Librarian of Congress, a strong supporter. Soon after, the person who had for better than twenty years occupied the position referred to as "Consultant in Poetry to the Library of Congress" became officially the "Poet Laureate of the United States." Warren's was the first such appointment, and the Library, along with the National Endowment for the Arts, set about planning a fete in honor of the great poet's installation, to take place in the spring of 1987, called "The Continuity of American Poetry."

In order to emphasize that continuity, each living former consultant was invited to sponsor a younger poet, whom the elder would introduce for a brief reading at the Library of Congress. The elder poets were, as you might expect, an impressive bunch: Sir Stephen Spender was there, Daniel Hoffman, Maxine Kumin, Stanley Kunitz, William Meredith, Howard Nemerov, Gwendolyn Brooks, Karl Shapiro, Josephine Jacobsen, Anthony Hecht, James Dickey, and more. The younger poets, if they were not quite so impressive a lot then, have become so over the years. There was Gertrude Schnackenberg, Michael Ryan, Edward Hirsch, Dana Gioia, Ellen Bryant Voigt, Naomi Shihab Nye, and E. Ethelbert Miller, among others. I knew the work of many of the poets there that night, elder and younger, but I'd never met a one of them. It was unlikely that I would have, living as I did far, far out of whatever loop poetry might be said to exist inside. A few of the poets in attendance that evening and over the next few days might even have visited Idaho in the past, as tourists, say, or if they had come as professional poets they had probably gone to Boise, the capital and the closest thing to an actual city in the state, or to Moscow, to the University of Idaho, where I teach now but did not then. I was very pleased to be among the younger poets sponsored, and I felt a little overwhelmed too—like a new kid in school, a little awkward, a little bashful. The rest of the poets all seemed to know one another. I didn't know a soul. My wife had come with me though, and so we stood off to the side for quite a while, munching extravagant canapés and watching name-tags.

Mostly what I watched for was James Dickey, who had sponsored me. Time for the ceremony, and the reading, got ever nearer, and still there was no sign of him. I was aware that evening that though I might well be the least widely known poet in the room, my sponsor poet was exactly the opposite. He was without a doubt the most famous, or infamous, poet in America. Everyone knew Dickey, or knew *about* him. He was brilliant and outrageous. He is sometimes said to have invented the contemporary poetry reading. The larger share of Dickey's fame and wealth no doubt came from the success of his novel *Deliverance*, and the film based on it, but he was also a poet of the highest order. Or had been. Nothing much that mattered seemed to have come from Dickey lately, but what existed already was often extraordinary. He could have rested on his laurels, I suppose. He had no intention of doing so, but he might have been better off if he had. What remained too much with us, and with him, was his persona: hyper-macho, philandering, drunken, egomaniacal. I didn't know much about him beyond his poems then, but I loved the poems. In my heart, as I stood there with my wife, feeling invisible and misplaced, I knew that I was there because of Dickey's poems, that my poems, my new book, existed because of what Dickey had already written.

Almost everyone who has been involved with poetry and poets over the last thirty or forty years has a James Dickey story, often some tale of drunken boorishness. In my informal accounting of such anecdotes, however, I've found that approximately every third story ends with something like "but he gave an incredible reading that night too."

Not long after Dickey's death, his son, Christopher, who had become a successful journalist, published a memoir about his father called *Summer of Deliverance*. It is an excellent book, as honest and generous as it could be, even as it never pulls a punch. There's a passage early on that reads as follows:

> So those times I got out of El Salvador or Nicaragua,
> Libya or Lebanon, feeling lucky to have survived and
> in love with the world, I could just barely bring myself
> to call him. We'd talk, but not much, and I'd say "I love
> you" when I said goodbye and "Fuck you" when the phone
> hit its cradle. What a shame, I would think, that I still
> loved him at all.

Perhaps the most moving part of the book is its conclusion, in which the weak and dying poet and his son reconcile. In those pages, James Dickey appears disarmingly human—vulnerable, regretful, fearful, loving.

A couple of years later, Henry Hart's massive biography of Dickey, *The World As a Lie,* was released. It's a useful volume, but finally I don't think very much of the Hart book. No doubt, this particular biographer's task was in some ways an unenviable one. A good deal of the latter portion of the book seems like little more than an *ad nauseum* recitation of Dickey's bad behaviors. It's seems clear, somehow, in the tone underneath the tone, perhaps, or in the seeming preoccupation with the nastiness—often to the exclusion of much relevant or penetrating discussion of the poetry itself—that Hart might have developed a profound distaste for this subject. It's understandable, in a way, but it is also unfortunate. Rarely, as I toiled through Hart's tome, did I feel that the biographer was drawn to his subject by love. Love of the work, I mean. The poems, at their best, are triumphant. A few of them (and for any poet "a few" makes for an enviable percentage) approach the level of masterpiece and may well attain it.

I'm going to talk about Dickey's poems as one who loves a lot of them. I believe every poet's reach should exceed his grasp, and Dickey, through a combination of extravagant talent and considerable hubris, reached in his fashion as high and far as most have. That he ultimately crippled himself with alcohol, that he let the hubris overwhelm the talent, is part of the tragedy that is the man's life. And it *is* a tragedy, I think, even a classical one. Because the poems, so many of them in his major volume, *Poems, 1957-1967*, validate that life too. Their accomplishment is what gives Dickey's time on earth as a writer its genuine nobility, a nobility without which, at least in classical terms, the life would not be tragedy but something closer to farce.

And speaking of farce, I do have my own Dickey stories to tell. That night in 1987, at the Library of Congress, Dickey did arrive. Finally. We were less than ten minutes from lining up and heading into the green room, and I was still huddled up with my wife to the side, when, for the first time—the only time—all evening, the white-bright lights of the television crew went on, and there he was. He was a big man, and he seemed to tower over the crowd.

I moved to the edge of the circle gathered there around him, the TV reporter, and the camera crew. Our eyes met. I hoped he might recognize me from the photo on the back of my book. He'd just provided a generous jacket quote for that book, my second. And when the lights went down, I strode directly to him and extended my hand.

"Hello, Mr. Dickey," I said. "I'm Robert Wrigley."

There were others waiting to introduce themselves or say hello, so I stood aside, but stayed close. He smiled. He was gracious. In a few more minutes we were all, senior and junior poets, gathered in two parallel lines, ready to head downstairs to the green room, and then to the auditorium's stage.

Once we were assembled, Dickey leaned toward me.

"All right, Wrigley," he said, "don't fuck up."

I remember I looked him in the eye for a moment or two before I spoke.

"No problem," I said.

"I want you," he said then, "to hit a shot at the buzzer, son. You hear?"

"Two point or three?" I said. I didn't miss a beat. The only problem was, he didn't seem to get it. Either he didn't hear me, or the long-range, three-point shot was something he'd forgotten or didn't know about. He looked puzzled, even a little irritated. I was about to explain my line, but just as I opened my mouth to speak we were called to silence and began our march downstairs.

In all I spent perhaps four hours with Dickey during those few days in Washington. Most of it was at dinner, after that first night's reading, and that dinner is the source of the stories I could tell that would have fit into Henry Hart's biography. When I ordered a Jack Daniels, he claimed he wasn't supposed to drink but ordered his own anyway, a double. The three of us also split a bottle of wine. By the time we separated and walked back to the hotel, I was angry, even a little disgusted. But I'm not going to tell those stories. Not here, not now. Maybe not ever. There are enough of them already.

At the end of this essay, I'll say a little more about that time. At this point, before I say some things regarding a few of Dickey's poems, I'm going to say a few words about myself and my relation to poetry and to this particular poet.

When I was an undergraduate student at Southern Illinois University in the early 1970's, I had two young professors who were particularly powerful influences on me. One was a specialist in American literature, particularly Southern literature; the other was a poet. Both had written doctoral dissertations on James Dickey. I suspect there were quite a few fresh Doctors of Dickey loosed upon the land in those days. Both of these men loved Dickey's poetry, and because I loved them—I was their apprentice, a novitiate—I wanted to love Dickey's work, too, but I didn't. Or rather, I couldn't. I tried some. I recall that I was intrigued by the then-and-still anthology piece, "The Heaven of Animals." I liked the situation of it, I think, just as I liked the situation of some others of Dickey's poems, like "The Shark's Parlor," in which the speaker recalls a time when he and a friend bait a hook "with a run-over collie pup" and go fishing for—and, I should add, *catch*—a shark.

But liking the situation of the poem is not the same thing as genuinely appreciating the poem. For reasons I would eventually begin to understand, I did not engage with Dickey's language. I did not love what he said, because I did not love—in fact, I did not even hear—how it was he said it.

Why? In part, I think it was Dickey's very Southernness that kept me from a full engagement. This was the last years of the war in Vietnam. I was twenty-two or twenty-three, freshly discharged from the army on the grounds of conscientious objection. I was, I felt, a fire-breathing, left-wing radical CO, and for me the South was George Wallace, Lester Maddox, Bull Connor, the murders of Goodman, Schwerner, and Chaney, and of Emmett Till; it was Jim Crow and lynchings; it was military hawks and hypocritical Democrats whose devotion to democracy did not extend to anyone who was not white.

This was not very thoughtful, of course. The same *ad populum* notions might have kept me at arm's length from Flannery O'Connor, William Faulkner, and Eudora Welty, among many others, but of course they were not at all like Dickey, really. The fact is, I sometimes think I was also suspicious of what seemed to me then an overwhelming Southern presence in American literature. My first poetry text in college was Brooks and Warren's *Understanding Poetry*. My British lit professor, a dapper and diminutive man, spoke with a lilting drawl and though he was teaching us Coleridge, could not resist pointing out that something from *Biographia Literaria* was, in his words, "not unlike that position taken by the Fugitives in this century." Of the Fugitives, I had read that they were "conservative," and that was all I needed to know in those days.

To make this case, I have to blame matters cultural, I have to point the finger outward, though the fact is, I was the problem. If I had not yet engaged with Dickey's poems, I could not expect that I would be moved and instructed by them, let alone that I might love them. It was only some years later, in the late seventies, after I'd finished my graduate degree, published a first book, and was a young professor in his first tenure-track position that my opinion of Dickey—indeed my whole relationship to poetry—changed.

That first book of mine was, more or less, my MFA thesis. I don't dislike it. There are poems in it I still feel something for, but it was apprentice work. By 1981, five years after I'd left the workshop, I was ready to make a leap. I was ready to take my art to the next level, you might say, but I was also teaching four classes a semester, mostly freshman composition; I had a very young son I adored in the midst of a none-too-stable—in fact, a coming-apart—first marriage. I used to complain that I didn't "have time" to write what I wanted, and while no doubt that was true, it is more accurate to say that I didn't *know* what it was I wanted to do as a poet. Something was missing from my poems. That much I knew. I certainly wasn't happy with what I was writing. It's a precarious place for a developing poet. Many aspiring poets just stop; some become stifled, dyspeptic, academic whiners, and if I'd kept on the way I was going then I shudder to think of the grumbling, embittered and unhappily tenured character I might have become.

What happened that changed my perception of Dickey, and that ultimately changed my life, was a visit to the campus where I taught by the poet Dave Smith. Also a Southerner, he was an especially hot commodity in the poetry world then, if that's not too much of an oxymoronic description. It was the early 1980's, and Smith's poems were regularly, if not weekly, in the *New Yorker;* he was in demand for readings and he seemed to be changing teaching jobs annually, in part because he was an exceptionally fine teacher. His first night on campus he gave a very good reading, and the next day he delivered a talk about the role of the writing teacher as mentor. It was a smart, insightful talk, I remember, though I honestly could not tell you much of what he said beyond the way he concluded. He finished up by reading a poem by James Dickey, a poem called "Mangham," in which a high-school geometry teacher suffers a stroke but goes on scrawling his elaborate proofs on the blackboard.

Hearing that poem was a revelation for me. It was not the first time I'd ever been in a room in which a poem of Dickey's was spoken aloud, but it was first time one of Dickey's poems seemed to enter into me; I heard it work. I was bowled over, stunned, pinned to my seat. What I heard—what Smith made me hear—was the poet's voice inside the poem. I heard the craft; I perceived, in my mind's ear, the art that made the poem a poem. Not just the idea of the poem, but the essence of it. I heard the unsayable said out loud, and from that moment on, every page—even until this very day—every poem I read on the page lives in my mind in a particular voice that is not Dickey's or Smith's, but my own, a voice I might never have clearly heard without them both.

At the end of Smith's lecture that day, I took him to the airport and bid him a very fond farewell. I was thrilled, and I'm sure he could see it. He and Dickey had done something to me. I couldn't wait to get home, and as soon as I did, I went straight to the shelf, pulled down *Poems, 1957-1967* and started reading.

Not every poem I read worked for me then, either. Some never will. Dickey's best work is often complex and demanding, but compared to my attempts at reading Dickey half a dozen years before, I was nailed. Every few pages or so I was dazzled; I practically bounced in my seat as I read. There is no other word for it—I was *high*.

When I read the following poem—which I'd read before, with my other, earlier, and inadequate ear, and missed—I had to stop and think. And also to breathe.

The Lifeguard

In a stable of boats I lie still,
From all sleeping children hidden.
The leap of a fish from its shadow
Makes the whole lake instantly tremble.
With my foot on the water, I feel
The moon outside

Take on the utmost of its power.
I rise and go out through the boats.
I set my broad sole upon silver,
On the skin of the sky, on the moonlight,
Stepping outward from earth onto water
In quest of the miracle

This village of children believed
That I could perform as I dived
For one who had sunk from my sight.
I saw his cropped haircut go under.
I leapt, and my steep body flashed
Once, in the sun.

Dark drew all the light from my eyes.
Like a man who explores his death
By the pull of his slow-moving shoulders,
I hung head down in the cold,
Wide-eyed, contained, and alone
Among the weeds,

And my fingertips turned into stone
From clutching immovable blackness.
Time after time I leapt upward
Exploding in breath, and fell back
From the change in the children's faces
At my defeat.

Beneath them I swam to the boathouse
With only my life in my arms
To wait for the lake to shine back
At the risen moon with such power
That my steps on the light of the ripples
Might be sustained.

Beneath me is nothing but brightness
Like the ghost of a snowfield in summer.
As I move toward the center of the lake,
Which is also the center of the moon,
I am thinking of how I may be
The savior of one

Who has already died in my care.
The dark trees fade from around me.
The moon's dust hovers together.
I call softly out, and the child's
Voice answers through blinding water.
Patiently, slowly,

He rises, dilating to break
The surface of stone with his forehead.
He is one I do not remember
Having ever seen in his life.
The ground I stand on is trembling
Upon his smile.

I wash the black mud from my hands.
On a light given off by the grave
I kneel in the quick of the moon
At the heart of a distant forest
And hold in my arms a child
Of water, water, water.

What I love about this poem is practically everything.

To begin with, it's something of a narrative poem, and it was Dickey who brought me to my fascination with narrative. Although, again, it's only "something of a narrative," in the manner of many of Dickey's poems. It tells the story from the point of view of a first-person narrator, in this case a lifeguard at a lake where children are swimming. The story's pretty clear. A child goes under, the lifeguard tries to save him and fails, and in the desolation of his failure he swims into a boathouse and hides there, unable to bear the look on the "children's faces / At my defeat." While he's hidden in the boathouse, night falls, the moon rises, and it is then, in the magical light of the risen moon, that he imagines yet saving the child, even more heroically, in this case bringing the dead one back from the other world, from death. He imagines himself "The savior of one // Who has already died in my care." He imagines himself a Christ-like figure, with the drowned boy as Lazarus, only to have to return from his imaginings to the reality of his failure again. That's the poem's story, but to get at its heart you have to go deeper; you have to hear, and see, a lot more.

The magic starts with the first line. It's the rhythm. It's perfectly anapestic in that opening line (some will argue that "lie" also bears stress, and perhaps it does, but the rhythmic context buries it). Bum-bum-BUM, bum-bum-BUM, bum-bum-BUM. It's incantatory, infectious, and while Dickey never enslaves the poem to the meter, those anapests are always there, the way a drum keeps the beat while a jazz player improvises. ("The LEAP of a FISH from its SHADow"; "i RISE and go OUT through the BOATS." He especially loves the trimeter line in this poem, opening with an iamb, then hitting us with the two powerful anapests.) In this case, the rhythm, established so early and never entirely out of earshot, is what gives the poem a great deal of its emotional power. This is a ceremony of the bereaved but hopeful spirit; it's a séance, a summoning. It's a dream-state with a beat. If you were going to try to bring someone back from the dead, to call to the other world, you'd not find a better, more ceremonial, more likely meter to call in than anapestic.

And what about that opening line? Why does Dickey call the boathouse "a stable of boats"? Lots of reasons. "Boathouse" is, first and foremost, a compound word, and like most compound words, it is a locution of convenience. It saves time, breath, and spit. And while poetry is driven by compression, not all compressions are created equal. "Stable of boats" may be twice as many syllables long as "boathouse," but it is also perfectly cadenced (STAble of BOATS; DAH-dah-dah-DAH), and built into the opening prepositional phrase and the line's concluding subject/verb/modifier, it rings in Dickey's signature meter.

But "stable of boats" does more than fill out the rhythmical line. If you think about it, in terms of diction, "stable" is wrong, or inappropriate at least. There's no other reference, anywhere in the poem, to stables or barns, horses or livestock. It's a metaphorical usage then, but what is its effect, beyond the sonic one?

It's mythological, almost a kenning. Calling the boathouse a "stable of boats" turns the boats into horses. I'm tempted to say "steeds," even, for this is, again, a poem that is concerned with aspirations beyond reality, beyond death. Its aim, at least for the purposes of the speaker, is to dream the impossible into being. And it's not, in this regard, at all far-fetched, since by stanza two, moving from mythological to Christian imagery, the speaker imagines himself actually walking on water. ("I set my broad sole upon silver, / On the skin of sky, on the moonlight"—walking on moonlit water, eh? How can you not love that?—"Stepping outward from the earth onto water / In quest of the miracle . . . . "

I might also argue that "stable" has intellectual resonances in the poem. Consider the word's derivation. From the Latin base *stare*, meaning "to stand," as in, of course, that place where the horses stand, or in this case the boats, standing at the ready. In the Old French *establir* it means "to establish or secure," which is precisely what the speaker means to do in his waking dream, which is not only to bring the boy back from death, but to reestablish order in the universe, which because of the drowning has collapsed into chaos.

I've hardly moved past line one, and I could continue for a good long while on the genius of the opening passage. The second line, for instance, the last half of the opening sentence, reverses the rhythm from the rising anapests of line one to a series of falling measures. Those three trochees (SLEEPing CHILdren HIDden") deftly reinforce the speaker's intent to stay hidden. By simple contrast, and via the line's feminine ending, the cadence here quiets the poem, as though the speaker, having swum into the boathouse, has now pressed his finger to his lips and said "ssshh."

In line four, there's that surprising (and characteristically Dick-eyesque) placement of the adverb *before* the verb it modifies, in which the lake is made to "instantly tremble." The effect is so obviously superior it hardly warrants discussion, but I will point out how this syntactical inversion places the verb at the end of the line, where its tremblings are more vividly seen and felt, and at the end of the sentence, where the period's pause sends the trembling out into the air behind the line. And it is also true that the three syllables of the adverb stretch the line out until it is the stanza's longest: I can almost see it trembling even now. Note, too, that "instantly" is itself a dactyl which, followed by the trochaic "tremble," suggests a kind of logical diminishment of a trembling thing as it subsides toward stillness.

The fact is, the voice I began to hear those years ago is the voice that I finally learned to read in. It's the voice that allows me to see and hear the effects and possibilities. I'm not talking about intents here, either; I'm talking about effects, an artful assemblage of effects that in their totality are almost invisible in the seamless poem, but which, isolated and examined, reveal their—and the poem's—artistic power.

The speaker in this poem sees, or imagines, his own mytho-logical transformation. "My steep body flashed / Once, in the sun," a vivid and dramatic, even a hallowing, image. And it is important to note here that the poem, at this point, has moved from the post-calamity hiding in the boathouse, back in time to the incident itself. The drowned boy is dead when the poem begins; the structure is a frame established in time: from the present to the past, to a kind of dream-like future-present, and finally back to the historical and tainted present. The memory of the boy when the speaker "saw his cropped haircut go under," is all the speaker has of him. And in memory, of course, the mythologizing must necessarily stop when that "steep body" has flashed "in the sun," for once the speaker enters the water he is blind, helpless, and doomed to fail. "Dark drew all the light from my eyes," he says. "I hung head down in the cold. / Wide-eyed, contained, and alone / Among the weeds." His "fingertips turned into stone / From clutching immovable blackness." The memory is horrible. "Time after time," he says, "I leapt upward / Exploding in breath, and fell back / From the change in the children's faces / At my defeat."

Though the drowned boy is lost and will be the subject of mourning, "The Lifeguard" is in truth an eponymous poem; it is the lifeguard's story—focused primarily on his suffering, his despair, his "defeat." In the poem's sixty lines, only fifteen are given over to a description of the drowning, and of those, all we, or the speaker, see of the drowned boy is when "his cropped haircut" goes under. At least, that's all we see in this life. The rest of the poem, up to the final stanza, exists in the *now* of the dream, the aspired-to myth.

At this point we are back at the beginning of the poem, where the moon rises and the speaker's "steps on the light of the ripples" are "sustained." The speaker calls "softly out," and the "child's / Voice answers." Notice it's not the child, but his voice that answers; it's a dream world, a never-never land, we're in. And sure enough, the child "rises," "patiently, slowly," until they are face to face, the dead and the living, the drowned boy and the failed lifeguard. In the penultimate stanza Dickey stitches back imagery and diction from earlier in the poem to unify and tighten, thus the boy when he rises comes "dilating to break / The surface of stone with his forehead." That surface of stone is stone because it is the dream surface the speaker stands on, like Christ upon the water, but it is also stone because, as we come to see, it is a surface that equally holds down the child as it holds up the speaker. Death reasserts its finality. And, of course, the only stone we see in the poem to this point is the stone the speaker felt his fingertips turn to as he clutched "the immovable blackness"—the blackness of death, of oblivion, and of mud. It is a subtle but highly effective strategy, which Dickey employs again with the use, again, of the word "trembling." Stanza nine is thus neatly stitched to stanza one. The miraculous, mythological man-sustaining waters that so vividly trembled in the opening stanza, come down in the end to the "ground," the water itself, upon which the speaker "stands." That ground is "trembling / Upon his smile." The dream, the visage that haunts; the guilt, the awful, immitigable remorse. Thus, in the final stanza, when the speaker washes "the black mud from my hands," we are taken back to the immovable blackness" that the speaker's "stone" fingertips found when he dived at first.

This concluding stanza likewise returns, more attentive than ever, to the poem's dominant meter, the anapest. Lines two and three are nearly lock-step anapestic trimeter ("on a LIGHT given OFF by the GRAVE / i KNEEL in the QUICK of the MOON"), and the poem's last two lines, so elegantly simple, so heart-breaking and bereft, are perfectly composed. "And hold in my arms a child," he says, with awful irony, giving us so late in the poem the ghost of an imagined success, only to tell us that it is a child "Of water, water, water." The water this time is insubstantial stuff. It holds no one up. The child is pure illusion, just as is the speaker's redemption, even as the anapests diminish from dominant in the stanza's second, third, and fourth lines, to a single medial anapest in line five, to a perfect strategic triplet of dying trochees at the end.

All this sort of hit-and-miss close reading means to do is to get at the lavish and skillful deployment of effects in Dickey's poem. It's not that the poems are busy or baroque; it's that they are complex and abundant with suggestion and connection. And most importantly of all, they are musical. This essay is necessarily truncated. I want to mention at least one other poem, and I've said nothing yet about the effect of all those prepositional phrases in the final stanza. I believe this effect is careful and studied, hauling us back, via a kind of poetical-syntactical unweaving, to a world so harshly embodied in the poem's last line. In a sense, that weaving and unweaving is something that enacts, approximately, the making and entering of the poem itself. Back in 1981, when I first entered this poem with my own voice in my ear, on the poem's own terms, it was simply the first of many such encounters with the exceptional genius of Dickey's work.

There are so many poems. This exercise I've given myself makes me ache for what I won't have time or space enough to praise. Among the masterpieces, in my taxonomy of Dickey's poems, is "The Firebombing," a poem that is horrifying, just as Dickey intended it should be.

"The Firebombing" is spoken by a man who was, as Dickey for years claimed he was but in fact was not, a night-fighter pilot. (Dickey was a flight radar operator and a very fine one and he did fly many combat missions and was decorated for them, just not as a pilot.) In the poem, the speaker is a man who dropped napalm on civilian targets in Japan near the end of World War II, and who, twenty years later, is unable to feel the slightest tinge of guilt for it. Published at the beginning of the U.S.'s bloodier involvement in the Vietnam War, "The Firebombing" was immediately and savagely attacked by a good many critics as a celebration, or a glorification, of war. The worst of these attacks came from Robert Bly, once a friend of Dickey's and an early champion of his work.

In fact, "The Firebombing" does not glorify war but speaks of its terrible contradictions, not just the celebration and joyousness of victory (these can hardly be said to enter the poem at all), but of the unspeakable detachment required of any soldier worth his salt. Dickey describes it in the poem as "the honored aesthetic evil," particularly the pilot's awe at the beautiful patterns of flame the napalm makes across the surface of the darkened earth. It's like fireworks reversed, the night sky inverted. The pilot in the night sky looks down on the patterns of deadly flames and sees only beauty. Because he cannot see the destruction he brings on, he does not have to face the horror of it. By this way is modern warfare made remote, even disconnected.

The fact is, I think one can make the case that "The Firebombing," by virtue of its very honesty, may well be among the most successful anti-war poems of the period (and there were a lot, most of them well-intentioned but utterly forgettable). In one sense, Dickey had in mind the worst sort of horror of modern war, the sort of war made possible by our long-distance "weapons of mass destruction," as they're called. (Or consider the even more distant detachment of what we're now using in the Middle East and elsewhere: drones.) We could kill and maim and destroy, but we did not have to see it at all. This detachment, in Dickey's mind, made the worst possible. It made, in fact, an ordinary American Everyman into a monster even he himself cannot imagine, because he cannot imagine what he did not see or what has not happened to him as something real. The challenge this poet gave himself was to write a poem that was both horrifying and beautiful. It is the beauty of the poem that makes horror of the situation more heightened. In the end, all the speaker can understand is being what he is—a suburban American man who, as the nation would have it, had done nothing but his duty.

I do not do the poem justice this way. No gloss can begin to lay out the levels of accomplishment and beauty of "The Firebombing." My point in bringing up the poem is two-fold. First, I mean to aim you toward it, so that if you do not know it already, you might go to it and see for yourself what dazzlements are there. And second, I mean to demonstrate to you that Dickey's poetic *modus operandi* is often one that knows, or accepts, no boundaries. He believed he could confront anything and make it into art. This is a position some will feel is hubristic and probably foolish on the face of it. I disagree. Don't go around announcing that there's nothing you can't do, but believe absolutely in what you do. Reach high and far. If you're not willing to believe, why should a reader? In a way, Dickey was the sort of man for whom we now understand the phrase "entitled white male" seems to have been minted, the likes, in truth, not seen since Hemingway, and maybe the kind of man whose likes began to die with our defeat in Vietnam; it's a death that continues in the twenty-first century, and ought to. But at the time of his greatest powers, Dickey was a poet willing to follow his imagination wherever it might lead him. And where are we willing to go in poems? I don't know. Is it a mistake to follow the imagination wherever it leads? I don't think so. All I know for certain is that I have been willing, for decades now, to let Dickey's poems take me where they will. And I have tried to learn to make poems that do the same.

I want to spend a little time with one more poem. It's hard to pick. The long "May Day Sermon" that opens *57-67* is amazing, a little Southern gothic grotesque, but mostly just amazing. I admire the audacity of "Falling" (suffused, and perhaps corrupted, as it is by its *very* male gaze), and the ironic sweetness of "Deer Among Cattle." There's the unlikely miracle of "The Sheep Child," the second half—the heart—of which is spoken by a being half-human / half-sheep from a jar of formaldehyde.

But I want to talk about a comparatively quiet poem.

A SCREENED PORCH IN THE COUNTRY

All of them are sitting
Inside a lamp of coarse wire
And being in all directions
Shed upon darkness,
Their bodies softening to shadow, until
They come to rest out in the yard
In a kind of blurred golden country
In which they more deeply lie
Than if they were being created
Of heavenly light.

Where they are floating beyond
Themselves, in peace,
Where they have laid down
Their souls and not known it,
The smallest creatures,
As every night they do,
Come to the edge of them
And sing, if they can,
Or, if they can't, simply shine
Their eyes back, sitting on haunches,

Pulsating and thinking of music.
Occasionally, something weightless
Touches the screen
With its body, dies,
Or is unmurmuringly hurt,
But mainly nothing happens
Except that a family continues
To be laid down
In the midst of its nightly creatures,
Not one of which openly comes

Into the golden shadow
Where the people are lying,

Emitted by their own house
So humanly that they become
More than human, and enter the place
Of small, blindly singing things,
Seeming to rejoice
Perpetually, without effort,
Without knowing why
Or how they do it.

It's as modest a poem as Dickey was capable of, in a way. It's a lyric poem with the flavor of a narrative. The story is less a linear telling than a kind of unfolding tableau, in which a family, sitting inside a screened porch on a country night, is cast outward into the wild world in the form of shadows. It is here, in this shadow land, that the humans exist "in a kind of blurred golden country," a magical place. Dickey loved this particular place: that zone where human and animal come together. He loved the edges, the margins, the dangerous, almost-too-far destinations. This is the place where "The Sheep Child" exists. It's a prayerful place even. The people in the poem have "laid down / Their souls and not known it." In a wonderful, slanted way, this is something of an ecstatic poem, in which human beings "become / More than human." (Dickey's notion of the poet was, as he said, as "an intensified man" who must of necessity feel more things and feel all things more deeply than other people. I would like to suggest that he meant "an intensified *person*," but I can't.)

There are the classic Dickeyesque touches. Note the almost King James cadences of the opening stanza. There's also that Biblical diction: heavenly, created, peace, souls, creatures, rejoice. Check out that adverb/verb reversal in the middle of stanza three, where a bug—or in Dickey's golden otherness, "something weightless," almost like a soul itself—is "unmurmuringly hurt." And consider the daring, really, of suggesting, just past the middle of the poem, that "mainly nothing happens," after which comes the following simple and beautiful line: "Except that a family continues." That's Dickey's vision in a nutshell. That we continue, that we go on; that life and death and the horrors and ecstasies of our lives are all part of the continuum of life on earth. It is with this vision in mind that Dickey insists that we are, that his "family" in the poem is, "more than human." We live our lives so often unaware of our spot, our role, our insignificant blip in the cosmos.

The real genius of the poem is, I think, its perspective. Where is the "eye" of the poem anyway? I have no doubt that Dickey remembered or saw at some point this very sort of scene. I imagine him rising from a family gathering—story-telling on the back porch, let's say—and heading out into the darkness. He was taking a leak, maybe, and when he turned to go back in, he saw some shadow gesture move across the dimly lit space, traced the motion back to the people inside and understood his poet's role, which was not only to see such a thing but to bring it to the page as the mystically powerful meditation that it is.

I find this poem to be stunningly beautiful. It contains the essential sadness of things, the lovely, bittersweet core of human life. It is a meditation on life's enormous ineffability. At the end the poem, after the family is "laid down / In the midst of its nightly creatures, / Not one of which openly comes / / Into the golden shadow." Those people "enter the place"—look at that dramatic, assertive line break. They enter the place! Praise God almighty, it is the place! And they enter it.

And when we see it is the place "Of small, blindly singing things," doesn't that place include the poet—the humble voice of the singer—as well? In some vital and essentially human way, the poet is the human being's soul-exploring point-person. Are we not all "small, blindly singing things"?

Notice the peculiar, and I think perfect, ambiguity of the last few lines. The people "enter the place / Of small, blindly singing things," and who or what is it that is "seeming to rejoice" there? Surely it is the "blindly singing things," of course, but it is also the human beings who now rejoice "Without knowing why / Or how they do it." They don't know why or how because they are mired in the human world, for one thing; it is only their shadows out here in the golden verge, after all. But even by virtue of their shadows they can be of the wild and perhaps truer world, especially if the poet is there, to note how effortlessly they seem to rejoice, even if—like any real poet—they don't know "why / or how they do it."

Finally, as much as anything else, I love that this is the same poet who might seek Christ-like powers in "The Lifeguard," or who would presume to speak for a creature half-human, half-sheep. This is a poet of the utmost poetic ambition, a man who can also approach such ambitions with modesty and quietude.

The next morning, after our strange dinner, I felt like a hypocrite, lugging my stack of his books upstairs from my hotel room to his for his signature. When he met me at the door, he was freshly showered; he smelled of cologne. He had on a double-knit polyester shirt. He looked like a banker headed out for a round of golf.

"My, you *are* a collector," he said. My stack of books was more than a foot high.

He sat on the bed and began signing the books, inscribing most of them. He wrote passages in Latin and German, asking me in each case if I knew what they meant. I didn't and it embarrassed me to say so, but he quickly translated and told me whose words they were. He was learned; I wasn't. He looked at me and smiled.

About halfway through the signing, he spoke, looking down at what he was doing instead of at me.

"I'm sure that I said some things last night that I ought to regret this morning." He said this quietly, without looking up. I didn't say anything back to him; I couldn't think what to say.

"I have to stop drinking," he said. "I really do."

Then he did look up at me, and there was a kind of half-grin, half-grimace on his face. He was ashamed. And I wish I had said more than I did, or said something. I was embarrassed for him, and for my inarticulateness too.

He nodded, then went back to signing. Neither of us spoke again until I left, when I thanked him again for his sponsorship. We shook hands then and said good-bye.

Now, of course, I wish I had told him face to face how much his poems meant to me. I wish I had told him how much I was moved and instructed by "The Lifeguard" or "A Screened Porch in the Country." And even why.

Later that night he gave his own reading, with a few of the other "senior poets," and he read only "new poems." They weren't very good, I don't think; certainly they were forgettable. Maybe he didn't really know they weren't good poems, though you have to wonder if that was possible. Much of the talk you'll hear about James Dickey will be about his great collapse, and I don't think it should be that way. There are poems in the body of his work that are amazing. There are poems—a lot of them—that I will always wish I had written. I wish I had told him that at least.

WHO LISTENS BUT DOES NOT SPEAK

Some years ago I offered a poem in a graduate seminar I teach now
and then called "Poetic Forms and Modes." I passed copies of the poem
around the table and I could sense, even before anybody said a word,
the students' reactions: the poem looks exactly—one is tempted to
say *anachronistically*—like what it is: an Italian sonnet. The reactions I
sensed were a species of world-weariness; they were graduate students,
after all, and mostly very young, and they were therefore a little jaded
and more than a little cynical. Here we go, they must have thought,
the sonnet. That old fourteen-line warhorse love machine.

The fact that the poem is a sonnet would matter, formally,
yes, but they were mistaken. I wasn't presenting the poem primarily
as a formal structure, but as a particular poetic mode: the dramatic
monologue. Yes, our study of it would also demonstrate the sonnet's
considerable flexibility (it's a little song that can tell a story or, in this
case, suggest even more), but I was especially interested in its dramatic
and situational complexities.

You note right off the quotation marks. The poem is a spoken
thing; a character speaks it.

I began the class discussion with another poem, perhaps the
most famous of all of Robert Browning's dramatic monologues, "My
Last Duchess." In Browning's poem the Duke of Ferrara speaks to
the representative of a Count, an emissary who is there to negotiate
the marriage to Ferrara of the Count's daughter. Everybody knows
this poem, or ought to. In fifty-two couplet-rhymed pentameter
lines, Ferrara makes clear to the Count's emissary that he had had
his "last duchess" killed. Why? Because "her looks went everywhere,"
because " 'twas all one! My favour at her breast, / The dropping of
the daylight in the West"; and because she had a heart "too soon made
glad." Therefore Ferrara "gave commands; / Then all smiles stopped

together." He's exceptionally cruel, Ferrara, an elegant and, though he coyly denies it, an eloquent monster. He confesses to murder, without actually confessing to murder at all.

Then I asked the students to imagine themselves as the Count's emissary. What would they do? What could have been this man's alternatives? Tell the young woman? Tell her father? And in the process slander Ferrara and cut his own throat? Browning's poem is the testimony of pure power, a power so absolute it could not be withstood. Ferrara could do anything he wanted, and he wanted this hapless functionary to know that. And to feel it. And the reader also feels it, not only Ferrara's demonic cruelty, but the emissary's hopeless knowledge.

Edwin Arlington Robinson won three Pulitzer Prizes for his poems; I believe only Frost, who won four, had more. Robinson has not fared so well as Frost in the years since, but he was, like Frost (who was twenty years or so younger than Robinson), an impeccable formalist. And it seems obvious to me that Robinson, like any poet, would be fascinated by the enormous tensions within Browning's great poem, most especially the presence of that other character on stage.

Here's Robinson's poem:

HOW ANNANDALE WENT OUT

"They called it Annandale—and I was there
To flourish, to find words, and to attend:
Liar, physician, hypocrite, and friend,
I watched him; and the sight was not so fair
As one or two that I have seen elsewhere:
An apparatus not for me to mend—
A wreck, with hell between him and the end,
Remained of Annandale; and I was there.

"I knew the ruin as I knew the man;
So put the two together, if you can,
Remembering the worst you know of me.
Now view yourself as I was, on the spot—
With a slight kind of engine. Do you see?
Like this . . . You wouldn't hang me? I thought not."

The first line contains three pronouns to be parsed: the third, I, is the easiest; it's the speaker. The first, "they," is, well, *them*, the culture at large perhaps, legal, moral, and ethical. You know the people he means: them. The third pronoun, the middle one, is the most troublesome: "it." This first line of the poem suggests that Annandale is an "it." By the final line of the first quatrain, however, that suggestion is revised and made clear: "I watched him," he says, "and the sight was not so fair." Annandale is, in other words, a man, although he is a man in very dire straits.

"I was there," says the speaker (twice) "To flourish, to find words, and to attend." He is also, in the list comprising line three, a "Liar, physician, hypocrite, and friend." And in the second quatrain, he tells us what Annandale, the man, was, taking us back to the opening line's "it": he was "An apparatus not for me to mend— / A wreck, with hell between him and the end." A man who has become a thing. The speaker is Annandale's friend and physician. The words this speaker finds, the ones that make him a "liar," are the words he offers to "them," or perhaps to Annandale, even to himself. Whatever has befallen Annandale, he is a doomed man, and the speaker's hypocrisy is perhaps both in the words of comfort he offers to Annandale (we'll get you through this, buddy) and to them, his auditor or auditors, perhaps the medical establishment (we'll try this; we'll keep him comfortable). These are his lies, or at least his first lies. Of course his greater hypocrisy is the violation of his Hippocratic oath: the sonnet's sestet is his confession—almost as deft as Ferrara's perhaps, but not so gloating nor smug. Rather it is his oblique and sidelong confession that he has committed euthanasia, that he has put his friend, Annandale, out of his misery ("with a slight kind of engine"—imagine a hypodermic syringe here, its piston and cylinder).

What I wanted the students in that class to consider was the audience or auditor in *this* poem. Who is our speaker speaking to? Given the final line, I have always assumed the auditor (or auditors) to be, perhaps, a police officer, a judge, maybe even a jury. We can't know for sure, but whoever it is, that person or persons now holds in his or its hands the speaker's fate. If you were that auditor, that cop, that judge, I asked the students, what would you do?

Robinson's poem consists of exactly 140 syllables. Ten contained and enormously expressive and somewhat—under the duress of the situation—cagey syllables per line. There are metrical substitutions but every line has its appointed five stresses. It's also worth noting that it is a wholly traditional Italian sonnet. Two rhymes through the octave (A and B), and three (C, D, and E) in the sestet. It's a little song of love about a mercy killing, and in that regard the fact that the poem is a sonnet is itself a potent irony. It may even be a poem primarily about love, a kind of awful love, but love nevertheless.

The students in that class were smart, progressive, open-minded souls. They were mostly millennials. A couple of them even hailed from states that have laws allowing what we now call "assisted suicide." They felt compassion for the speaker. They found his sidelong not-quite confession of his crime moving. At least at first they did. One or two of them finally lit upon the poem's final line, and it is the poem's most problematic. What, they wondered, was implied by that opening elliptical phrase, "Like this . . ."? Someone imagined the speaker holding up a hand and pantomiming the working of a syringe, as though "like this" was a visual demonstration of the means by which Annadale's demise was accomplished.

But almost immediately another brought up the ambiguity of this line's first pronoun, a demonstrative one: "this." What if that "this" was not referring to the pantomimed injection, but to something else? To the speaker's situation, maybe.

They were getting pretty heated by this time. What do you mean, someone demanded? What else could "this" be? Surely it was the pantomime! No, surely it was the situation!

The answer, as far as there could ever be an answer, was in the rest of the line.

The central syntactical unit of the line is a question. The speaker is asking, and his question is made, as it is all through the poem, directly to his auditor or auditors: "You wouldn't hang me?" How does one decipher the tone of that question? And what is the tone of the speaker's response? That is, what is the tone of his response, both to his own question and what we might take to be the auditor's silence or inaction? "I thought not."

Is the tone a kind of smugness, the kind almost worthy of Ferrara himself? Or is it something else? Yes, of course. We might like it to be one or the other, but it is both. Consider: at this point in the poem, it might be said that, if there is a man who is suffering, if there is a man who might be called "a wreck, with hell between him and the end," might it not be the speaker himself? This self-identified liar, physician, hypocrite, and friend? And how might *he* be mended, this physician who has killed, and who has killed a friend?

Is it possible the delicacy of his confession, which is never really a confession at all, is a kind of plea? "I thought not" may then suggest the speaker's disappointment as well as his satisfaction. He has done the right thing and in doing the right thing he has made the darkest of marks upon his own soul. As he knew "the ruin as I knew man"—Annandale, in other words—this auditor knows him. (His peers, a fellow citizen.) "So put the two together, if you can, / Remembering the worst you know of me," he says. He's pleading for understanding here. Is he asking for understanding when he inquires "You wouldn't hang me?" Is he asking the auditor to hang him? To mend him in the only way he found to mend Annandale?

Other phrases might be seen to support this position. That "if you can," for example. Knowing the enormity, and the enormous guilt, of his own actions, the speaker may already know the auditor can probably put the two—the ruins and the men—together. But the next step is momentous and terrifying: killing him. And after all, the speaker's "ruin" is psychological and spiritual, not physical. His pain is not a body's pain and is, therefore, more abstract. Then there's line twelve: "Now view yourself as I was, on the spot." Like the sentence before it, this one's imperative (Ferrara dispenses imperatives too), but "on the spot" is itself almost abstract. "On the spot" is an idiom that suggests two contradictory conditions: one is either on the spot and therefore perfectly placed to do the right thing; or one is on the spot and therefore in a very difficult, perhaps even impossible, situation. As the speaker was "on the spot," so now is the auditor, and similarly ambiguously. What is the right thing to do in this latest difficult situation?

I'm simply suggesting that poem's final phrase, "I thought not," is not Ferrara-smug at all, but resigned. The hell between the speaker and the end is one he will have to suffer through, uncondemned but equally, if differently, doomed. In this case, the courage (if that's what it was) that he possessed in the face of Annadale's suffering, is a kind of courage the auditor cannot, or will not, muster.

I think the mark of this poem's genius has everything to do with the ambiguity of the poem's situation, and even more in the way it is rendered in a monologue. I think it also has to do with the brilliant reversal of the roles of power. If in Browning's poem Ferrara is all-powerful, and if, in his absolute power, he condemns the Count's emissary to silence and to the terrible knowledge that power has imparted, then the situation is wonderfully opposite here. It's the auditor who has the power here but who cannot, or chooses not to, employ it.

As one student in that class a few years ago pointed out, in a way the same sort of curse that Ferrara put upon the Count's man, Robinson's speaker has now put upon the auditor in the Annandale poem: that is to say, the auditor now knows about a killing, and the auditor's choosing (or being unable) to do anything about it, is a curse the auditor too will have to live with for the rest of his (or their) lives, just as will the emissary of the count.

Writing is about life, but it really isn't like life. Nobody likes problems in life much, but writing is always a problem, one you create, almost happily. The poem's a breathing machine you find a use for. What addicts you to writing is the problem of its difficulty. If it were easy to do it well, there wouldn't be much reason for doing it at all. The best poems sniff out and find complexity, the complexity of being a living human possessed of a soul. Such poems can engage with all manner of ethics and morality, with life and death, and with life-and-death decisions. E.A. Robinson, his reputation so long in eclipse, was sometimes very good at that. The fact that it is impossible to determine the precise tone of the poem's final line is part of its richness, and the poem—spoken by that guilty speaker—manages to place at least part of its moral and ethical burden upon the auditor: he who / she who listens but does not speak.

What we love about poetry at this level—which is to say, at the level of literature; what we should understand about this poem and Browning's poem—is that we, the readers, are also implicated somehow. We are also the auditors, for the time of the poem and its momentary aftermath. We can enter into this situation, we can experience the tensions and complexities of what's going on around us while we're inside it. Then, of course, we can walk away. Or maybe not. Poetry shapes our neural pathways. If the poem does what it's supposed to do, we can walk away, but we will not, or cannot, forget.

THE GIFT

February, 1990. I had a ten-week-old baby boy at home, only recently discharged from the hospital. He'd been born six weeks prematurely, with a shock of black hair and a case of jaundice so severe his skin was the color of English mustard. But now we'd had him home for two weeks, and he'd been ensconced in a fiberglass blue suitcase—a portable set of bilirubin lights. He wore a pair of cotton goggles, attached to adhesive Velcro patches on his temples, and a preemie diaper. We kept a fire roaring in the living room, so as to keep the temperature above 80 degrees, and for two full weeks one of us, my wife or me, was up with him, twenty-four-seven.

Eventually, he was fine, his dark hair lightening by the day, his skin gaining its normal color. He was nursing more or less constantly then too, and sleeping in a bassinette by our bed. Things, as much as they do with a newborn in the house, had returned to normal.

We were due to move to Missoula come March, when I'd assume the Richard Hugo Chair in poetry at the University of Montana, for the spring quarter, and I was to teach a graduate course there, on two poets whose work meant a great deal to me, James Dickey and Sylvia Plath. It was an odd pairing, I admit, though I called them, for the purposes of the course, two "poets of extremity." Regarding Dickey, I felt sufficiently prepared, but not so with Plath. Therefore, with my wife's blessing, I loaded up the old Jeep and drove south into the Craig Mountains, my backpack crammed with four days of food and drink, and a good twenty pounds of books (Plath's *Collected Poems*, and a stack of critical texts), then skied the seven miles in to the cabin we had there in those days.

There was no electricity or plumbing at the cabin. A big wood stove for heat, a propane cook stove and propane lights; lots of candles; an outhouse. I melted snow for water. We'd been making such winter trips to the cabin for years by then, so it was all familiar to me, although I'd never gone in alone, and all the work I'd planned notwithstanding, I was there no more than an hour when I found myself terribly lonely and depressed, missing my family, if not the ordinary comforts of home.

Actually, loneliness and depression turned out to be a pretty good mood in which to approach Plath. That seems counter-intuitive, no doubt. You might think—I certainly would have—that Plath's searing, angry, desperate, and majestic poems might just make such an emotional state deeper and darker. But no, it was just the opposite. The critical articles kept me interested, and the poems excited me in ways they never had before. The first day and night, I read the entirety of Plath's poems, then all through the next two full days there, I read and read and read criticism about them, and about her (I had Edward Butscher's *Method and Madness: A Biography,* as well as Anne Stevenson's *Bitter Fame,* published just the previous year; I'd read Linda Wagner-Martin's biography at home, in the last weeks before our son was born). By the second night, I'd relax after dinner and sip whiskey, put the secondary texts aside, and go back to the poems.

Some poems I read six or eight times, making notes in the margins, drawing lines between connections, sonic and meaningful. I also brought along a cassette recording of Plath reading her then-recent poems (from the last autumn of her life, in 1962), along with a BBC radio interview with the British writer Peter Orr, on a program called "The Poet Speaks." In one of her responses to a question, Plath half-apologizes for her American voice. "I think that as far as language goes," she says, "I'm an American, I'm afraid, my accent is American, my way of talk is an American way of talk, I'm an old-fashioned American." But in fact her speaking voice, both in the answers and in the poems, seems halfway-Anglicized to me, and her enunciations are extremely crisp and British-seeming. I would slip the cassette into the little player we kept at the cabin, and even from that pair of small speakers, her voice seemed to body forth into the room. It was invigorating. I seemed to have taken a back-country Idaho ski trip with a ghost.

We know from the biographies that during those miraculous months in the fall of 1962, that Plath was rising at 4:00 a.m. to write for a few hours until her children woke, around 7:00, she said, at which point she assumed the role of an ordinary mother through the rest of the day, as day by day, she wrote the poems that she herself said "would make [her] reputation." As they did. It's possible to read the poems of that fall as a kind of hyper-lucid and incendiary suicide note. At some point in the Montana term to come, a student would wonder aloud if it wasn't, in fact, the poems that had killed her, in a way. I understand how the student could wonder such a thing, though it's probably just as likely that the poems, and her children, were what kept her alive and thriving (the nature of that thriving is certainly debatable) for her last months.

What is eerie and unnerving, reading those poems, is the sheer force of their emotional content. It's hard to talk about, strictly as craft, as art. It's hardly possible to speak of Plath's prosody and diction as something separate from her life. No, that's not true. One can speak of the poems as made things, without referring to the agonized consciousness that made them, but as it was with me in the cabin those days and nights, Plath's ghost, for lack of a better term, is always right there. The poems *are* that consciousness enacted as poetry of an exceptionally high order, but the ghost, of course, is the problem. We wonder, how much of one's response to the poems is actually one's response to the mythology that has come to energize and surround that ghostly presence? It's not an answerable question. Or it's not one I care much about, even as I admit the near-constant presence that accompanies my reading of the poems.

Consider October, 1962. On the first day of the month, Plath wrote a poem called "The Detective." (The dates of composition here are those listed in *The Collected Poems*.) Through the next four weeks, on an almost-daily basis, she wrote an additional 24 poems. Twenty-five poems in a month. Apparently she did not write any poems on the 5th, 8th, 13th, 14th, 15th, 22nd, 23rd, 26th, or 28th, though the notations in the *Collected* also say that she worked on one of the poems, "Lady Lazurus," from October 23 through October 29, so perhaps the 26th and 28th were productive days as well. Among the poems Plath produced in October 1962 were "Ariel," "The Applicant," "Daddy," "Cut," and "Nick and the Candlestick," just to name a few.

Kind of mind-boggling, isn't it? Where does this kind of—forgive the word again—productivity come from? Surely Plath was manic. In a kind of amazing ragged-edge, full-speed-ahead, damn-the-torpedoes, holy-shit, what-hath-poetry-wrought *zone*. She was, let's admit it, inspired, possessed, and inhabited by the muse. I like to think, given that she had but a few more than a hundred days left to live, that during these weeks she was as absolutely alive as she had ever been.

I want to talk about just one poem from that October. There are so many that strike me now as superb compositions, but this one . . . well, it has always seemed among the most haunting of the poems from that time. I'm not going to bother trying to keep the ghost out of the commentary that follows. It cannot honestly be done, I don't think, not by me.

On October 27, Plath wrote two poems. Let's say the first (if the *Collected* is correct) was "Ariel." It's an astonishing, emblematic, totemic kind of poem. A poem of transcendence and of transcendent vision, it would have made any poet's day. Or career. But she wasn't done that day. (Remember, again, that she was writing no more than those three hours each early morning.) I imagine her reading over "Ariel" one last time and putting it aside. She might have looked at the clock then and thought, there's still time for another, a short one. This second poem is the one I want to talk about.

"Poppies in October" is only twelve lines, the majority of them short, from as few as three syllables long to as many as fourteen. It would have been still early morning. Plath might have looked from her window to see not only the poppies of the title but the woman and the ambulance spoken of in the opening stanza. If there is a narrative attached to this poem, it's all in that first stanza. The rest is contemplation, interrogation, and terrified introspection.

POPPIES IN OCTOBER

Even the sun-clouds this morning cannot manage
    such skirts.
Nor the woman in the ambulance
Whose red heart blooms through her coat so
    astoundingly—

A gift, a love gift
Utterly unasked for
By a sky

Palely and flamily
Igniting its carbon monoxides, by eyes
Dulled to a halt under bowlers.

O my God, what am I
That these late mouths should cry open
In a forest of frost, in a dawn of cornflowers.

I don't think there is a poem among that October's that better illustrates Plath's sense of herself in those days as "a peeled nerve," as a kind of medium for the energy and terror of true inspiration. The sun is barely risen. The morning's clouds are lit by it, glowing deep red-to-pink, but the color, those reds, are nothing when compared to the petals of poppies. These are the year's final blossoms probably. The petals are very much skirt-like, so the metaphor is a simple visual trope. And yet, we understand such an image is deployed for more significant reasons. Plath had been betrayed and left (some would say abandoned) by her husband. She is alone with her two small children in an apartment in London; that mother-work, a full-time-and-a-half job in the best of circumstances, is made all the more difficult by the absence of her husband.

If she had also seen a stricken woman taken away in an ambulance, rather than a man, say, that too would have seemed consistent with her sense of being deeply, almost mortally, wounded. The woman's "red heart" blooms beyond the poppies' blossoms. Red, the color that symbolizes lifeblood and love. Also rage. And the color of that imagined heart "blooms through her coat," as though Plath, with the most vivid hypersensitivity, could see right into her. It's the adverb that amazes though. That stricken woman's heart blooms for Plath "so astoundingly." It is itself a kind of miracle of seeing and fellow-feeling, or as Plath the poet puts it, "A gift, a love gift / Utterly unasked for." She was at a point in the month and in her life when everything that showed itself to her was the stuff of poetry, even as everything she saw vitally connected to her and to her understanding of her situation as both a poet and a woman.

It's interesting to note that either it is the sky that fashions the gift it presents to her, or that it is the sky itself that has not asked for such an enormous sensitivity and ability as Plath has taken on. (Hasn't she herself asked for it? Isn't that the poet's relentless seeking after inspiration?) This is such an ordinary, if beautiful, morning sky, "Palely and flamily // Igniting its carbon monoxides." The sun, given the autumn clouds and urban smog, is pale, but its effects are like fire. What an ingenious line "Palely and flamily" is. It's metrically regular: a double dactyl, and perhaps it is only coincidental that neither my computer spell-check nor the OED can deal with the word "flamily." Just as it is, surely, an even more coincidental fact that the only difference between "flamily" and "family" is a single L, though for Plath it might have seemed that it was indeed her family that had gone up in flames.

That the sky is "Igniting its carbon monoxides" suggests a species of poisonousness residing in those "eyes / Dulled to a halt under bowlers," in the way that the ordinary world keeps on going about its business in the face of the poet's awareness, as well as her electrified suffering. It's a moment when the poem manages to indict those who are numbed to the spectacular beauty of the world (those poppies, that sky), and thus to the kind of peeled sensitivities required of the poet. It also brings in, as counterpoint to the skirts and the woman in stanza one, the metonymic figure of those "bowlers." Dull men, in other words. Men, to be sure.

The conclusion of the third stanza is also a kind of dead end for the poem. The poppies and the woman, all through the first two sentences, are meant to be understood, in all their metaphorical and literal values, as things of which only someone in the condition of one such as Plath could be aware. Don't you see? Don't you see how everything I see leads to the reignition of my misery? But would it be better to be dull? To *not* see so much more deeply into the significance of things?

The poem's final stanza expresses this particular agony, and thus the strange ecstatic horrors of Plath's situation. After the long second sentence, strung across eight of the poem's nine lines to this point, the full stop and the silence between stanzas rings with something like . . . well, *waiting*. Now what? What does it mean that I see such things and make of them this sort of sense beyond sense? Then she asks, "O my God, what am I?" The agony in that line is palpable. She's not wondering who she is, but what. As though to have gone where she has gone and to feel what she has felt and was feeling, is a kind of monstrousness. And some would say that Plath's behavior, including her suicide, has a monstrousness about it.

And maybe it is monstrous, this concentrated and ravishing sensitivity, or more likely, what it leads to in the life beyond or behind the work. It looks a lot like madness, like van Gogh's, or maybe even, more contemporaneously, Frank Stanford's or Joe Bolton's. It's a romantic delusion, surely, to think that such artists have somehow gone to depths or extents that other great but more stable practitioners do not attain. Such a mania cannot, I wouldn't think, be something one could cultivate. More likely it's just a chemical imbalance. We can honestly wonder if anti-depressants might have kept Plath alive and writing for decades more.

What *was* Plath at this point, in late October, 1962? If she were a character in my son's NBA video game, her every drive on the basketball court would be trailed by flames. She was on fire. She was in another place. She had left the rest of us behind. She felt more than most of us ever will for any reason.

Still, strangely, despite the despair of her inquiry in the final stanza of "Poppies in October" there's something in the poem's final two lines that is, while still deeply sad, a kind of reaffirmation. "What am I / That these late mouths should cry open," she says. The skirts of stanza one are mouths now, and crying open. There's something we should understand as beautiful here, something Plath herself understands as beautiful. She is seeing into the heart of things, into the very thingness of things. How these "late mouths" have entered into an especially brief and even truncated season. How they will not last long, coming to blossom in a "forest of frost" that will wilt and kill them heedlessly and without malice but surely dead. And how in their brevity and ordinariness they will most likely go unseen and unacknowledged by those who might see and take note of them and their beauty. Also how the world goes on when one or another of us has fallen—that stricken woman; how this is what must be, and how for some it is the going on that simply cannot be accomplished. Perhaps those "late mouths" may also be understood as Plath's children, wakening around seven a.m., probably hungry; it was the moment when Plath had to stop wondering what it is she was and become what she had to be: a mother.

The poem's final image I take to be yet another example of skillful metonymy. The cloudy and smoggy sky has become the blue of cornflowers. Another day worth living through—she had, it would turn out, only 116 more left to live fully through—has arrived. The children are to be looked after and loved.

One more thing, perhaps, again, coincidental. October 27th was Plath's birthday. She wrote two magnificent poems on the day she turned thirty. That must have seemed to her, even in her state of mind, itself a kind of gift.

Every day of our son's early life was also a gift to us. Even when we finally brought him home, he had to be taken back to the hospital twice daily for a blood test to check his bilirubin levels. A pediatric nurse would use a razory lancet to poke his exceptionally tiny heel, then draw the wee-est dram of blood into a glassine tube. Of all the bad parts of those days, this was the worst. A very placid baby otherwise, he suffered those regular cuttings and wailed as though his heart were broken. My wife simply could not face those twice-daily trips to the hospital, so it fell to me. The last few days, I cried too, every time he did, and the nurses too seemed heartbroken and offered us both their sympathies. But by the time I'd rebundled him in his blanket, nestled him in his carseat, and gotten him home, he was fine again. For all he knew, this was just what living was: something regularly hurt you and then it was all right again, until the next time.

Up there in the cabin in the Craig Mountains, I listened again and again to Plath reading "Poppies in October," and I thought of my son at home, with his mother and sister and brother. By then, whatever it was that caused him to be so treated was over and gone, and of course he has no memory of those times. After the last blood test, I carried him out into the cold winter weather. He was already asleep. The sky was brilliant blue, and the sun, though not warm, was astounding.

NEMEROV'S DOOR

"Isn't this your life?" —RICHARD HUGO

You think you might begin this story with an admission: you really don't know who you are, or who you were, or how you became the one after the other. Or others—it's not as if you've only been two versions of yourself. And what does it mean to have become? How is becoming accomplished? Maybe it's about time. From time to time, there are portals. You step through and become, or you don't. How much control over these things do you really have? You wonder if the self is a matter of becoming at all, or if it's just something that happens to you. How would you know the difference?

But instead, you'll start with this, which is a fact: you can fix in time much of your father's history, and therefore your family's and your own, according to your memory of what car he was driving at the moment, although it isn't always easy. Once, with your mother and sister, you tried to remember all the cars he'd bought and sold. The three of you lost count around ninety-something; there were just too many, although you in particular had a knack for remembering details ("Yellow and white '57 Mercury with a bad case of rust and pushbutton drive" you said, and your mother remembered). In this way, you're like your father, insofar as he too has an eye, and a memory, for detail, although his adoration of automobiles is not something you have come to share. If the car gets you there and back, you're fine with it. You maintain your cars mechanically, but you do not wash them very often. This has always been beyond your father's understanding.

The strangest car your father ever brings home is a 1950 Dodge two-door sedan. He bought it for $50. Someone has repainted it a hideous yellow. With a brush. Your mother is speechless. "But it runs good," he says. The next day he gives it to the woman across the street, whose husband has recently died; she and her daughter are without transportation.

This is in 1967. It is unthinkable to him that the remnants of a family now fatherless should be without a car. None of you ever really knows the neighbor man except by sight, the occasional wave when you're coming or going. Then the neighbor man is gone for good. His daughter is the same age as you and your sister.

For most of your early life your father worked two jobs, the first as a civilian employee of the Air Force. (He had his own airplane once and was just a few hours shy of his pilot's license, when, in 1950, his wife became pregnant. With twins. He was twenty-eight. That was the end of that.) The other job was selling cars. This second job—on weeknights and Saturdays—brought in extra money and probably taught him a lot about socializing and making conversation. He had been a very shy young man. You gather from your mother that your father, in his young manhood, did not have a great deal of self-confidence around other people. Until he did. You can understand that. You remember what that's like. In regards to selling cars, your mother knew it would be good for him, being out in the world and having to talk with people he did not know.

Selling cars also gave him the means to buy cars, and it turned out he was very good at both parts of that bargain. The owner of the local Mercury dealership he worked for was an old friend—like him, like every other man of your father's vintage in those days, a World War II veteran. Your father bought his cars at cost; sometimes he'd take them back to the lot a few weeks later, having "fixed them up." Often a month would pass during which there would be three or four different makes and models in the driveway in almost weekly succession. Your mother seemed occasionally irritated by it but yet allowed his obsession. (Cars were cheaper than airplanes at least.)

But on the day you're remembering, your father is retired from both of those jobs. These days he builds, repairs, refinishes, restores, and re-upholsters furniture, in a shop in his basement. And he drives his favorite car ever: a 1975 BMW 2002. If there is another BMW in the small, southern Illinois town he lives in, you've never seen it. Your father came to German cars via the Volkswagen. Your census determined that he's had at least ten different VWs—six Beetles, two Karmann Ghias, a Squareback, and a Campmobile; you may have missed a couple (should you count the Audi, you wonder?). Of all those nearly unnumberable cars, the BMW is his baby. He dotes over it. He will own it for more than two years before it is driven in the rain. That seems a strange thing to be proud of, although he is. In some unaccountable way, so are you.

And now it is you who are twenty-eight. It's 1979. You're visiting from Idaho for Christmas, and you and your father are flying down I-70 west toward St. Louis, at a silken eighty miles per hour. He draws your attention to the purr of the BMW's engine as you go. He always does that. You're on the way to Left Bank Books, at the west end of the city, not far from the campus of Washington University. Your parents have given you a $50 gift certificate. They know you'll want poetry, and they'll leave the selection of titles to you.

It's late December, a Russian front sort of day, windy and spitting occasional dry snow, mid-to-upper-teens. Your father finds a parking place right out front. This matters. He likes being able to keep an eye on his car, and he's guessed correctly that it will take you quite a while to make your picks.

You love bookstores the way your father loves car lots. You love the smell of books the way he loves the smell of a new car. There's a substantial poetry selection at Left Bank, and poetry books are especially important to you. On this day, you pick out no more than five volumes in all. You would have gotten more but one of them is a thick hardcover: *The Collected Poems of Howard Nemerov*. The book had won both the Pulitzer Prize and the National Book Award the year before. And Nemerov is a local poet. He's been teaching at Washington University for years. You admit that it is probably the awards that prompt you to buy such an expensive book ($20), since at this point you really only know one of Nemerov's poems.

While you study the poetry shelves, your father wanders the bookstore, spending most of his time in the World War II history section. He collects books about the war, especially books by Ernie Pyle, or about the air war. He probably buys one today; you're not sure. He calls World War II "the good war," well before Studs Terkel's book of that title. You think he means it only a little bit ironically.

After leaving the bookstore, you cross the street to a diner for lunch, which is where you mention to your father that Howard Nemerov had been a pilot in the war, and that he teaches over at Wash U. This makes the poet vastly more interesting to your father—the pilot part, at least—although you suspect your father too is impressed with the prizes emblazoned on the cover of Nemerov's book. Somehow he might be thinking that this is an opportunity, some possible sidelong entry into a part of the world you mean to join, a world in which you publish books that win big prizes. He knows it's good to meet people. Sometimes they can help you. Or maybe he thinks he might play a part in helping you get there, wherever it is you're going. He might be thinking, "You're aiming to be a poet, right?" (You think you already are.)

So he suggests you head over to Washington University after lunch, to see if you can find the poet Howard Nemerov.

"It's semester break, Dad," you say. "He's not going to be on campus."

"You never know unless you try," he replies.

You split a Reuben sandwich and each of you has a cup of some kind of dark, rich soup with barley. Maybe there's a poster on one of the diner walls depicting Lou Brock stealing a base. A common enough thing around St. Louis. You've been a St. Louis Cardinals fan off and on (but mostly on) since your childhood. Your father, on the other hand, has never understood baseball, or any other sport, for that matter. He understands cars and airplanes and work. He has never seen the point of games. You wonder if poetry too does not seem to him some sort of game, a way of saying something by not exactly saying it at all, or by saying something else. You understand why he might think that, although you never ask him what he thinks about what you do. You know he's proud of you, although it seems that he understands your obsession no more, and in some ways perhaps a lot less, than you understand his.

When he was a very young man, your father, with virtually no education, figured he'd have to find a way to buy an old truck and make a living hauling away trash for people. This was the late 1930s, deep in the Great Depression; he could not imagine any other possibilities for himself. But then the friend of a doting and resourceful aunt somehow finagled him a slot in a government-sponsored aircraft maintenance course, at Parks Air College, not far from his hometown. It is, he says, after meeting your mother, the luckiest thing that ever happens to him in his life. It is a portal he steps through.

After lunch, your father pays the tab then steers the BMW in the direction of Washington University.

You remember reading the one poem of Nemerov's you know in an anthology five or six years before. There were other Nemerov poems in that collection, but if you read them you do not remember them. This one is called "The View from an Attic Window." It's elaborately formal, but somehow the formal intricacy doesn't put you off the way it does in so many other poems of the time (rhyme and the counting of syllables and/or stresses is something it will take you a few more years to truly hear and thus to cotton to). What affects you most about the poem is its subject really, and its point of view. The speaker is a man looking back on an experience from childhood, and there is something about that boy's experience that makes you feel as though it was exactly like your own.

"The View from an Attic Window" is a poem about mortality. Or rather, it's about intimations of mortality, about the moment when a boy comes to an unbidden awareness that everyone—everyone he knows and loves, everyone everywhere, even he himself—will die. When did you become aware of mortality? You don't remember. There must have been such a moment, when you realized that, yes, your father and your mother, for example, would die, like everyone else, including yourself. All you know is, from the first time you read Nemerov's poem, it seemed that that moment had surely been like the one the poem describes.

So now you reread the first part of "The View from an Attic Window" (it is arranged in two numbered sections):

1

Among the high-branching, leafless boughs
Above the roof-peaks of the town,
Snowflakes unnumberably come down.

I watched out of the attic window
The laced sway of family trees,
Intricate genealogies

Whose strict, reserved gentility,
Trembling, impossible to bow,
Received the appalling fall of snow.

All during Sunday afternoon,
Not storming, but befittingly,
Out of a still, grey, devout sky,

The snowflakes fell, until all shapes
Went under, and thickening, drunken lines
Cobwebbed the sleep of solemn pines.

Up in the attic, among many things
Inherited and out of style,
I cried, then fell asleep awhile,

Waking at night now, as the snow-
Flakes from darkness to darkness go
Past yellow lights in the street below.

There is nothing about your child's life that resembles that of
the boy in the poem. You never had a house with an attic, at least not
one large enough to hold a lot of "inherited" things. Let alone with a
window. Then again, despite the foreignness of the setting, the situation strikes you as universal. Besides, it's not the place as much as the
situation: a boy, alone, coming to a terrible and terrifying awareness.
And it's also the voice: the words of an adult man—precise, formal, rich
with detail and allusion—that capture the archetypal and convincing
sadness of the boy's realization. It's a knowledge that, once known,
can never be unknown again. At first, in the opening section, the boy
just seems sad; perhaps he's merely lonely, and his crying is born of
what he himself is uncertain about. Anyone who has managed to live
the entirety of a child's life without ever being unaccountably sad
about something has lived a very charmed existence indeed. Maybe
it's solitude itself, the proximity of alone to lonely, the sense that the
absence of your family—even if they are merely elsewhere in the same
house—suggests a loss, even an abandonment, never to be overcome.

When your father was eleven or so, he was sent to spend a
couple of successive summers with distant relations on the other side
of the state. How it was he traveled from Collinsville, just east of St.
Louis, all the way to a farm near Clay City, not far from the Indiana
line, you don't know. Neither of his parents ever drove a car. The reasons for this relocation were, according to family lore, two: he was a
"sickly" child, and it was thought that fresh air and farm work would

do him good. The second was that his own family was profoundly impoverished. He was the eldest of three children; it was 1933 or '34. His coal miner father was out of work. In photographs from the time, your father is extremely skinny; he looks malnourished. At least on the farm there would be plenty to eat.

But what was that like? Exile? Banishment? Did he miss his parents? His younger brother and sister? You remember three stories he used to tell of his summers on the farm. One made him laugh in the telling. He'd learned that if he used his slingshot to pop a pebble off the old plow mule's rump, the animal would leap in the air and fart prodigiously. If that seems cruel to you now, you remember the other stories. Your father told of watching the man, the farmer, beat a milk cow bloody with a two-by-four after she kicked her milk pail over. Your father could hardly bear to tell the story, but he did, regularly, and it always ended the same way. That man (Fritz Minnie was his name) wound up dying of some sort of agonizing cancer of the mouth. Your father believed there was some connection, possibly some direct cause and effect, between the man's cruelty to animals and his awful fate, although your father has never believed in God.

The farmer's wife on the other hand (you do not know her given name; your father always speaks of her as "Miss Minnie") seemed to be someone he might have loved. You suppose it was in those years on the farm that your father learned about mortality. In the third story he would tell, he spoke of Miss Minnie handing him a wooden crate of newborn kittens and telling him to take them out to the pump, fill a bucket, and drown them. He went out dutifully and filled the bucket, but he couldn't do it. There were five of them, he said. Their eyes were not yet open. Miss Minnie must have been watching from the kitchen window, because soon she came out, and keeping your father close at hand, showed him how it was done. One by one, she picked up each kitten by the tail and dangled it in the water until it drowned.

And this is the part of the story your father could not get over, nor could you, when he told it. The kittens would struggle some, and as they did Miss Minnie spoke to them in what he said was her tenderest tone of voice.

"There, there," she said. "I know, I know. It will all be over soon."

You are not exactly sure what any of this has to do with Nemerov's poem. Perhaps it's nothing more than the way these two boys—one, Nemerov's character; the other, your father—come to be aware of mortality. Nemerov's boy comes to his realization intellectually, by reading the signs and portents in the attic around him. For your father, it seems to have been drowned kittens. You can't remember when you first heard your father tell the stories of his summers on the farm, though you're sure it was long before you were a man. Somehow in all of this, you are yourself, and you are also your father, and Nemerov's boy in the attic.

By now, you have read many of Nemerov's poems, and this one remains the poem you remember, and admire, most, although you're not exactly sure why, or not exactly sure you want to know why. Part of it is simply that the poem moves you deeply—it always has. And that worries you, in some way. Sometimes it seems that you have been trained, that you have trained yourself, to regard the possibility of being moved by a poem as a little bit suspect. Does the poem ask for a deeper emotional response than it earns? The fear of sentimentality, this is. What would your father make of that? He was a lover of sloppy and sentimental movies.

It also worries you that you have tried and failed—on several occasions—to write a poem about your father's memory of Miss Minnie and the kittens. No, that's not true. It doesn't worry you, but you're puzzled by it, puzzled by your failure; it seems ready-made. In one version, the poem's main character is your father; in another, it's Miss Minnie herself. You are able to imagine, you think, what it must have been like to be your father as a boy, but you believe you're also able to imagine being Miss Minnie. Was she offering your father a lesson about the realities of farm life or of life in general? Sometimes you have to see things? You have to fight in a war? You have to drown cats?

You haven't given up on the possibility of a poem. Not yet.

There's also this detail: it was your father's chore, afterward, to take the carcasses out and throw them on the manure pile behind the barn. Likewise, he couldn't do that, exactly. He took a pitchfork and dug a little grave in the side of the pile and buried them all together.

You read the second part of Nemerov's poem.

2

> I cried because life is hopeless and beautiful.
> And like a child I cried myself to sleep
> High in the head of the house, feeling the hull
> Beneath me pitch and roll among the steep
> Mountains and valleys of the many years
>   That brought me to tears.
>
> Down in the cellar, furnace and washing machine,
> Pump, fuse-box, water heater, work their hearts
> Out at my life, which narrowly runs between
> Them and this cemetery of spare parts
> For discontinued men, whose hats and canes
>   Are my rich remains.
>
> And women, their portraits and wedding gowns
> Stacked in the corners, brooding in wooden trunks;
> And children's rattles, books about lions and clowns;
> And headless, hanging dresses swayed like drunks
> Whenever a living footstep shook the floor;
>   I mention no more;
>
> But what I thought today, that made me cry,
> Is this, that we live in two kinds of thing:
> The powerful trees, thrusting into the sky
> Their black patience, are one, and that branching
> Relation teaches how we endure and grow;

The other is the snow,

Falling in a white chaos from the sky,
As many as the sands of all the seas,
As all the men who died or who will die,
As stars in heaven, as leaves of all the trees;
As Abraham was promised of his seed;
    Generations bleed,

Till I, high in the tower of my time
Among familiar ruins, began to cry
For accident, sickness, justice, war and crime,
Because all died, because I had to die.
The snow fell, the trees stood, the promise kept,
    And a child I slept.

You don't know if your father, during his summers on the
farm, slept in a bed or on the floor, or if he had a room, perhaps in
the attic. You wonder how he slept that night after the drowning of
the kittens. For years, when he tells the stories, he becomes, for the
time of the telling at least, melancholy. Once or twice, it almost seems
that he might cry but he never does. He shakes his head in wonder or
sadness or both. He says, "the poor old man." You wonder about that.

In the poem, the trees, which teach us "how we endure and
grow," are the one thing, and the snow, that "white chaos from the
sky," is the other. One is life and one is time? Such a reductive reading,
and yet accurate, to a point. You wonder what it would have been like
to lead your father through Nemerov's poem, to teach him how it
might be read. Would that have been a good thing? What would he
have thought about the assertion that "life is hopeless and beautiful"?
You imagine him listening, and considering, then saying something
like, "Huh. Well, no shit." Could you have found a way to explain to
him that the poetry is not in what the poem says but in how it says

what it says? That sometimes the work of poetry is to tell us what we already know? Could you have explained that poems were a little like cars? Almost any car—even a badly hand-painted old Dodge—would have gotten you across the river to the bookstore and back. Fuel, engine, transmission, and tires. Words, lines, figures, and imagination. They are not all equal.

The campus of Washington University is nearly deserted that day, although you find a woman who aims you toward the building where the English Department is located, and the building is (strangely, it seems to you) unlocked. There must be a directory in the entryway, for soon you and your father are climbing a staircase and heading down a half-lit hallway toward Nemerov's door.

If there is anything on the door—cartoon, witty quote, a poem, the usual sorts of things seen on professors' doors everywhere—you don't notice it. Probably there's a nameplate. But you hesitate. You're nervous. Why would Nemerov be here now? It seems pointless. And there may be something else too. Embarrassment? Is it because you are there with your father, which would seem to make you as much child as poet? What kind of poet goes around meeting other poets with his father in tow? Is it more than that? This isn't something you would want your father to feel you feeling, but you think you feel it: *What*, you wonder, could your father possibly talk about with Howard Nemerov, the poet?

Well, airplanes, for one thing. Or World War II.

And what about you? Poetry? You're pretty sure you know which of you—you or your father—could better hold up his half of a conversation.

So there you are, hesitating, when your father says, "Go on. Knock."

Years later you cannot separate the picture of Nemerov on the cover of his book—brush of mostly gray hair, thoughtful look on his face, his glasses held in his right hand just before his chin—from the figure you see when the door opens. There he is, just as in life. Or just as on the cover.

"Mr. Nemerov," you say. "I wonder if you wouldn't mind signing your book for me?" You hold out the book like an offering.

He doesn't say a word but opens the door to let you and your father in. He rolls his chair back to his desk (what's on the desk? why don't you notice?), signs the book—no inscription, no date, just a signature on the full title page—then returns it to you.

"I'm a poet myself," you say. "I've just published my first book."

If you'd known you were going to meet Howard Nemerov, you might have brought along a copy to give him. But in some way you are also glad you didn't. It is so slender, so slight. A seedling, a Matchbox car.

"Congratulations," Nemerov says.

"This is my father, Arvil Wrigley." You will realize later that you never mention your own name and Nemerov never asks. They shake hands, say hello, pleased to meet you, or something like that.

Then silence, until you say, "Well, thank you very much," and Nemerov nods. He seems ready for you to go. You think you should say something about "The View from an Attic Window," but you can't imagine what it might be. Somehow every word of the poem is unavailable to you now. So you say goodbye, and you and your father back out the door and it closes. (Was Nemerov at work? Had you interrupted a poem?)

"He seems like a nice guy," your father says.

When you get back to the BMW, he takes up Nemerov's book to look at the signature, which is in black ink, slanted slightly right and highly legible. Your father approves of that.

He slips a cassette into the BMW's tape player. He'd had the cassette player installed a year or two before and found the plastic bezel that held it tacky-looking, even offensive, in the otherwise impeccably appointed BMW dash, so he disassembled it all and reinstalled it, this time mounted in a beautifully finished piece of cherry wood.

He's put in Lionel Hampton. He knows you'll like that. The two of you say little on the way back home. It's a nice drive though, the wind and snow notwithstanding. It's the snow that makes you remember the snow in Nemerov's poem. Could you have spoken about that, you wonder? You think to yourself that snow is always a symbol—it was born that way—and you know what it's a symbol of, even this particular snow, blowing across the interstate.

Although he is just two years younger, your father outlives Nemerov by better than twenty years, a full generation, but for most of his last decade and more, your father's life is afflicted. He is diagnosed with Parkinson's disease late, around his 80th birthday. A man with such very skilled hands, even until the onset of the disease, he is for most of those last years someone, as he puts it, who "can't do anything anymore." His power tools sit quiet in his shop. There are days when he insists he's going to work, and your mother has to sit barricading the door to keep him from the deadly stairs. In the last year he can still hobble to the john, but it takes him a while. Sometimes he doesn't make it. He reads, but mostly newspapers. He can no longer read books; he forgets what's happened from one chapter, or even one page, to the next. He still likes, as your mother says, to "look at" magazines about airplanes or cars or working with wood; he remains a subscriber to *Aviation History*, *Car & Driver*, and *Fine Woodworking*. She offers him a copy, and she always asks the same way: "Do you want to look at your airplane magazine?" "Would you like to look at *Car & Driver?*" Occasionally she just hands him one: "Here, look at your woodworking magazine." It doesn't matter if the issue is a new one or an old one. If he's looked at it before, he doesn't remember.

But for some reason your father never forgets the trip to see

Nemerov. When you visit in April 2014, four months before your father's death, you remind him about it.

"He seemed like a nice guy," your father says.

You're trying to figure it out—that trip, that day. It seems that you were some kind of intermediary between two men of similar age and similar historical experience. There is something about the fraternity of WWII veterans that made them what—equals? Is there a similar brother- and sisterhood of poets? You are the child of one of these men but sort of a drive-by acolyte of the other (it's no longer the prizes now; it's the poems). And yet, you have always had the sense that your father meant to deliver you to another world that day. It felt like a passage. This has, you're sure of it, something to do with the poem, and with your long awareness of mortality, including your father's. That night years ago, after the day you met Nemerov, you read, in the guest room of your parents' house, "The View from an Attic Window" again and again and again. The more you read, the more you saw that its art is in how its attention to a commonplace assertion—that life is hopeless and beautiful—is made not merely meaning but poetry. Something like magic is in that, although in truth it is no more than poetic engineering. Not all poems achieve what might be called "the condition of poetry," that point at which the words on the page are more than the words on the page. What would it have been like to try to explain such a thing to your father?

Then again, he likes to tell you, very few automobiles are man-ufactured to such precise tolerances as the BMW.

All that's between you and Nemerov is poetry. All that's be-tween Nemerov and your father is the good war, and maybe airplanes. Nemerov came from wealth and privilege, your father from abject poverty. Nemerov graduated from Harvard; your father did not quite finish the fifth grade in a degraded former coal-mining town. Did you mean to be like Nemerov? Only insofar as you meant to be a poet. Did you mean to be like your father? You're not sure you can say how it is you're like him even now. The kinds of things you notice or remember? That you make things? That you fix things? Poems, mostly. You're fairly sure your father has read all of your books; if he has ever read poems by anyone else you would be surprised. Why would he? For your father, poetry is the kind of thing his son writes.

You have a picture taken during that same April visit, a few months before your father would die, in which he's holding—reading, it appears—your then-new book of poems. (It's your tenth; your father must be astonished that you have so much to say about whatever it is you're saying). You never talk about your poems with him. Not ever. You understand that he doesn't know what to say about them, and you don't want that to embarrass him. But why don't you help him? Why didn't you? Which is more difficult, you wonder: learning to read a poem or learning to fly an airplane?

Still, there's the picture, your book in his hands and a look of concentration on his face. He's giving it a try. You love the picture, but for reasons of his illness, and probably more, he looks a little uncertain. Then again, it is hard to be where he is just then. And who. It is not clear how much he remembers about many things anymore, not to mention what those things might mean. And there is that sense he has probably always had, that what the poem is saying is somehow only part of what he should be able to understand but for some reason can't and, it seems, never could. Something in you knows this is only partly true.

Four months later, you make another visit to Illinois. Your mother knows it's time, and when she calls, you come. The first couple of days, your father is lucid but in considerable pain. You take your laptop to him in his bed and show him videos of Fred Astaire and Eleanor Powell dancing. He loves that stuff. You show him YouTube videos of fighter pilots and bomber missions in World War II. Those keep his interest for a while and keep his mind off his pain. For all its inevitability, it seems it is still very difficult to die. He watches the videos, but mostly he's transfixed by the laptop itself. What a sleek and fascinating machine, so beautifully made. He can't keep his hands off it. You call up pictures of 1975 BMW 2002s. You ransack photo albums in order to show him pictures of as many of his cars as you can find. That takes a couple of hours.

On the third day, hospice recommends morphine and sedation, so the next morning he is, at best, semi-conscious, if only barely. You sing him a couple of songs as he lies in the hospital bed, in the bedroom of the house he has lived in for more than forty years. You sing "Making Whoopee" and "My Buddy." You know what he likes. You wish you'd brought a guitar. You read him a couple of your poems too, ones that have to do with him; all of your books are on a shelf in that room. By the second day of end-of-life medication, he is continuously asleep or, more accurately, unconscious.

In the midst of a lengthy sit alongside his bed, you speak softly but directly into his ear. (You find you can't take your eyes from his ear; it is wrinkled and very beautiful. You even take a picture of it. Just his ear.)

You say, "You're close to the end, Dad, you know? But Mom and Kitty and I, we're going to be OK. We're all here. We love you, and we're all going to be OK."

You wonder if he might have whispered something similar to his own dying father, more than four decades before, although that seems unlikely. Something about generations and genealogies, about certain things that just aren't, or weren't, spoken. Language for your father and for his father too, no doubt, is and was above all a practical tool, for the transmission of information. You could make an argument on behalf of the practicality of poetry, but you don't really know how much you would believe it. Could you have ever explained to your father that yes, poetry is practical, but that calling it practical somehow demeans it? In your case, is it poetry, or is it the passage of time, that has made you able to say what you've just said to him? How in the world have you come to believe so much in words?

What you want to do is to give your father permission to let go, if he can.

You should have asked him, earlier on, when he could still speak, if he knew what had become of the neighbor woman he'd given the old Dodge to. You counted the Dodge in the census, although he owned it for fewer than twenty-four hours—that must have been a record. What might have become of her daughter? (You remember she had red hair; her name was Frances.) Are these people part of an intricate genealogy of your own, part of a genealogy represented by your father's relationship to cars, of all things? Would you have remembered the Dodge at all, if he had not made a gift of it? And what does it mean that you know there is a poem in the details of this memory?

Nemerov's boy watches the falling snow from his perch in the prow of his house, while you seem to be standing in a used car lot. Most of your father's many cars are junk now, or spare parts. Midway through the seventh decade of your life, your memories of your father are abundant and various, although you think it would please him to know that so many of the recollections you have of him are those connected with his cars. That would seem appropriate to him. But this place, this time, this ride, this car; this poem, this snow, this man named Nemerov, a poet, and you and your father: What is the significance of these several kinds of thing?

You're sitting alongside your father's bed, thinking about it. Your father is not his cars; will you be the sum of your poems? Do you write your way toward identity? Or away from it? You make a note to yourself to reread Eliot's essays. Though they were born fewer than twelve miles apart, it is unlikely your father has ever known who T.S. Eliot is. So what? But even here, sitting alongside your father's deathbed, you find that your own mind comes back to poetry, unbidden. Poetry has changed the way you think and feel. In your father's dying brain, among the clouds of sedative and morphine, what is happening? How

117

is his brain processing its own demise? How is it processing the things you say or sing? Another bride, another June. A bed is a bed, the light is the light, a car is a car, a word is just a word. Isn't it?

At some point near the beginning of those last days, you could have read your father "The View from an Attic Window." Given the circumstances, and the memory, that too would have been appropriate, you think. If you had, you would have reminded him of meeting the famous poet; that you'd driven to St. Louis in the BMW; that off and on it was snowing; and that it was he who delivered you to Nemerov's door and bid you knock.

You would have said "Nemerov was a pilot, remember?" And there you would have been again, in the shared memory of that car, that bookstore, that diner, and then that dimly-lit hallway and more. Now here you are, awaiting the inevitable. You could have told your father what the poem was about and why you admired it. But you didn't. What weighed more: the fear that he would not understand or the fear that you couldn't make it clear?

You wait. You all wait. As far as you can tell, your father is not afraid.

From a few yards away, outside the bedroom door, you hear the ticking and chiming at each quarter hour of a clock your father made years before. Each sculpted piece scrolled and mitered to perfection; a crowning finial turned beautifully on a lathe; the swirling cherry wood finished just right. You're amazed by the skill such a making must have required. Will Nemerov's poem outlast it? Will any of yours?

But you can't see the clock now. You can only hear it, and you wonder if your father hears it too: the tick-tock ratcheting of days, the accumulation of seconds, and the diminution of them too. Counting up, counting down. You think about that. Even now, in this waiting for the end, you could tell him those ticks and tocks are symbols, and if he could hear you, if only he could speak, you're certain he would tell you he understands. Of course he does.

It's four p.m., August 1, 2014. Your father will die in a little over four hours. Somewhere on earth, in the mountains of the southern hemisphere, at least, almost certainly, snow falls.

SOUL SINGING

In the autumn of 1973, I had a stack of poetry books checked out from
the library at Southern Illinois University-Edwardsville, where I would
complete a BA in English the following summer. The stack of books
(all of them those familiar slender volumes) was about seven times
the height of the meager pile of poetry books I actually owned. This
pained me. I was enamored, enraptured, and swept away by poetry. All
I wanted to do was write poems. I stole as much time as I could from
my studies to do so, but it wasn't enough for me. If I wasn't writing,
I wanted to be reading poems, and I wanted to be reading poems by
poets writing now, which is to say, within a decade or so of 1973.
Those poems were not what I was reading in my classes. The Lovejoy
Library at SIUE had a very good collection, but I wanted my own.

On the other hand, I was twenty-two, I'd exhausted my GI Bill
benefits, and books of poems were—or so they seemed then—expensive. The first book of poems I ever spent my money on was Robert
Bly's *Silence in the Snowy Fields*. I bought it used, at Centicore Books,
in Ann Arbor (its previous owner, one "Keith G. Bovair," signed his
name, in ink, on the inside cover). I paid $1.80 for it. The cover price:
$2.45. Paperback. The second, W.S. Merwin's *The Carrier of Ladders*, I
bought new, also in paper: $3.95. I couldn't afford it, but I was amazed
and puzzled and endlessly fascinated by Merwin's poems, so I splurged.

In order to find the poets who might have written books I
would want to spend my money on, I had the library. And I had two
anthologies. The first of these was from Penguin, edited by Donald
Hall, and called, blandly, *Contemporary American Poetry* ($1.50). The
book was published originally in 1962; my version (I still have it) is the
"Revised and Enlarged Edition," from 1972. The work of thirty-nine
poets is included in this enlarged edition. Among them are four women:
Denise Levertov, Anne Sexton, Adrienne Rich, and Sylvia Plath; and
two black men: Dudley Randall and Etheridge Knight. The remaining

thirty-three poets are white men. Looking at the table of contents now, I have to wonder why Robert Hayden was not included. Donald Hall taught at Michigan in 1972; Hayden had graduated from Michigan and taught there several years before heading to Fisk. This is a glaring, even a disturbing, omission to me today. In 1973, it was not. In 1973 I was not yet aware of Robert Hayden's poems.

The other anthology was The *Contemporary American Poets*, edited by Mark Strand and published by New American Library in 1969 (another $1.50). It included most of the poets Hall had chosen, but Strand's featured the work of ninety-two poets, including twelve women (only a slightly higher percentage than Hall's)—Levertov, Plath, Rich, and Sexton again, with the addition of Elizabeth Bishop (how on earth was she left out of Hall's?); Isabella Gardner; Louise Gluck (who would have been just twenty-six years old and have published just one book in 1969); Barbara Howes; Carolyn Kizer; Lisel Mueller; Constance Urdang; and Diane Wakoski.

Among black male poets, Strand selected, like Hall, just two, but not the same two. In the Strand, you find LeRoi Jones (Amiri Baraka) and Al Lee. No Knight, no Randall, and again, no Hayden. Also—and I have to admit, this seems bizarre to me now—no Gwendolyn Brooks, neither in the Hall nor in the Strand. Brooks won the Pulitzer Prize in 1950, the first African American woman ever to win a Pulitzer; she would not die until 2000. Even I knew about Gwendolyn Brooks in 1973. I was Illinois born and raised, nearly 300 miles south of Chicago, it's true, but still I knew, in high school, that she was the poet laureate of the state and that she was clearly *important*. That she is included in neither of these anthologies is beyond my understanding. And yet, of course, it is not. It is American history, and history has a way of afflicting the culture and its art.

The seventy-eight remaining poets in Strand's anthology, as far as I can tell, are white men.

Today—May 14, 2016—I find these proportions, and these

representations (or lack thereof), surprising. And not at all surprising. Did I read the poems by the four black poets in the Hall and the Strand? I did. On the other hand, in 1973, had I read much of anything by any writer of color? I'd read *The Autobiography of Malcolm X* the summer after high school. I'd read Eldridge Cleaver's *Soul on Ice* and N. Scott Momaday's *House Made of Dawn* in the army, in 1971. I'd read Baldwin's "Sonny's Blues" in a class. (I don't think I've ever quite gotten over "the very cup of trembling," once the professor explained the reference; I was Biblically illiterate then.) I'd read Brooks' "kitchenette building" in another class. That's all I'm sure of. I hadn't read Toni Morrison (*Sula* was published in 1973) or anything by Hayden yet, not even "Those Winter Sundays."

Poets, based on the evidence I had at hand, were pretty much all white men. If I saw anything unusual about that, I don't remember. I had crawled out of the lower middle class with my white male privilege fully formed, even as I was almost completely ignorant or in denial of it. I believed that I hated racism, but what did that mean in my life? My mother was one of the few members of my family's elder generations who did not use the N-word with alarming regularity, and she was outspoken about her fierce disapproval of it, so much so that, eventually, you never heard it at family gatherings (and I'm very proud of her for that). I had black schoolmates, but none of them would have been called friends. We were friendly toward one another, but I never visited a black schoolmate's house, and none of my black schoolmates ever visited mine. I had a secret crush on a black girl in high school, but we hardly spoke, for reasons I understand and am bewildered by now. Then again, this is the first mention of that crush I've ever made to anyone except my wife, so perhaps I'm not as bewildered as I think. I loved the Reverend King. I think I remember crying when he was assassinated, but that might have been Bobby Kennedy. 1968 was a brutal year.

I'd been drafted in early 1971 and discharged after a truncated nine-month stint. I was closing in on a bachelor's degree, the first in my family. By the fall of 1975, I would be halfway through graduate school, in Montana. I might have owned twenty-five books of poetry by then. I'm guessing that if there were twenty-five poetry books on my shelf, probably twenty were by white male poets. Bly, Merwin, Wright, Kinnell, Strand, and Hall; for some reason, I have a hardcover of Paul Zweig's *The Dark Side of the Earth*, which I still love (at $6.95, it was surely the most expensive poetry collection I'd ever bought). By white women, I'm sure of Plath's *Ariel*; Sexton's *Live or Die*; that might have been it. Also a copy of Gwendolyn Brooks' *Selected*. And a single book by a black man, just one: *Belly Song and Other Poems*, by Etheridge Knight.

I read Etheridge Knight's "The Idea of Ancestry" in the Hall anthology in 1973. It's a poem of great power and also possessed of a kind of supreme calm in the face of that which most of us would imagine as unbearable: incarceration. It wasn't much later, however, in the fall of 1974, my first term in graduate school, in Missoula, when I heard the poem read aloud. Not by Knight (not yet), but by Galway Kinnell. Kinnell began his reading ("The Bear" and four or five cantos from *The Book of Nightmares*) with "The Idea of Ancestry." He told us a little about Knight before he read the poem. I remember he said the name twice: "Etheridge Knight. Etheridge Knight," and nodded to the audience. We were to understand this poem, and this poet, meant a great deal to him.

If it was odd, hearing Kinnell say the first line or so—"Taped to the wall of my cell are 47 pictures: 47 black / faces"—I don't remember thinking so. I do remember thinking the poem was amazing. It seems to me now that it would have had to have been amazing, since I have remembered Kinnell's reading of it for over forty years. There's also this, regarding the rest of Kinnell's reading, consisting of those cantos from *The Book of Nightmares*: much of the time I am willing to say that *The Book of Nightmares* is one of the greatest American poems of the twentieth century, but of the four or five cantos he read that afternoon, I can only remember him reading one for sure—the first, "Under the Maud Moon." I bought a copy of *The Book of Nightmares* that afternoon, but I went home and found Hall's anthology and re-read "The Idea of Ancestry."

What I loved about "Under the Maud Moon" was the lavish and wonderful musicality of it. Some of it's almost (almost?) over the top. He's describing the birth of his daughter, Maud: "and she skids out on her face into light, / this peck / of stunned flesh / clotted with celestial cheesiness, glowing / with the astral violet / of the underlife." Celestial cheesiness? the underlife? astral violet? But I loved it then and I love it still.

On the other hand, here's the opening stanza of Knight's poem:

> Taped to the wall of my cell are 47 pictures: 47 black
> faces: my father, mother, grandmothers (1 dead), grand
> fathers (both dead), brothers, sisters, uncles, aunts,
> cousins (1st and 2nd), nieces, and nephews. They stare
> across the space at me sprawling on my bunk. I know
> their dark eyes, they know mine. I know their style,
> they know mine. I am all of them, they are all of me;
> they are farmers, I am a thief, I am me, they are thee.

Nothing over the top here. Nothing close. I spoke above of the "supreme calm" in Knight's poem, and this stanza exemplifies that calm. (Do you need to be told that Etheridge Knight spent eight years in prison? That he was wounded in the Korean War and wound up addicted to heroin? That he snatched an elderly woman's purse, in order to feed his habit, was arrested, convicted, and given a ten to twenty-five year sentence? That a white man would have received a shorter sentence is certain.)

The poetics here are spare and restrained. All the lines are more or less of a similar length; there's not so much tension created by the line breaks as a kind of particular attention devoted to the words that matter most. The closest thing to a figure of speech is the way the faces "stare" from their photographs "across the space" of the speaker's cell; the most meant-to-be-heard piece of sonic manipulation is the "me / thee" rhymes of the last two lines. What tension Knight creates here comes from simple syntactic and rhythmic parallelism: "I know / their dark eyes, they know mine. I know their style, / they know mine. I am all of them, they are all of me; / they are farmers, I am a thief, I am me, they are thee."

What this series of parallel statements does is set up the principle tension of the poem itself: that the "idea of ancestry," in this context, stretches across a particular continuum from freedom to the lack of it, from them to me. The poem is an expression of love, of shame probably, of enormous calm sadness, and of despair that will be survived.

It's very difficult to offer such a reading as the first sentence in the previous paragraph provides. That is, the idea of "freedom" as part of the idea of ancestry. It is especially difficult to contemplate the harrowing limitations on the "free" part of Knight's family in mid-twentieth century America. And it is corrosive and heart-breaking to contemplate the legions of African American ancestries today—in 2016—disrupted and even destroyed by the republic's continued institutionalized racism, here in this, our prison-industrial complex. The number of American citizens in prison now is appalling; the number of African-American men in prison is devastating, unjust, and implicates almost everything about the nation. It undermines the assertions of the republic's documents.

Maybe for Etheridge Knight there was freedom and then there was "freedom." I don't know. I have to hack my way through some awfully heavy privilege to even approach the front edge of understanding, but I'm trying. Knight said that he died in Korea from a shrapnel wound and was resurrected by heroin, then died from a prison sentence and was resurrected by poetry. All I know for sure is that the poetry that saved him has blessed me.

Here's the rest of the poem's first section:

> I have at one time or another been in love with
>   my mother,
> 1 grandmother, 2 sisters, 2 aunts (1 went to
>   the asylum),
> and 5 cousins. I am now in love with a 7 yr old niece
> (she sends me letters written in large block print, and
> her picture is the only one that smiles at me).
>
> I have the same name as 1 grandfather, 3 cousins,
>   3 nephews,
> and 1 uncle. The uncle disappeared when he was
>   15, just took
> off and caught a freight (they say). He's discussed
>   each year
> when the family has a reunion, he causes uneasiness
>   in the clan, he is an empty space. My father's
> mother, who is 93
> and who keeps the Family Bible with everybody's
>   birth dates
> (and death dates) in it, always mentions him. There
>   is no
> place in her Bible for 'whereabouts unknown.'

In the midst of all the plain exposition of this section, one notices certain eccentricities of expression. Numerals rather than numbers written out in script—a kind of shorthand, they speed things up; they give the stanza a kind of zip. And there are those regular parenthetical elaborations too. These serve more than anything else to characterize the speaker, although they're also deftly accretive, you might say. Again, they build tension; there's a progression from purely informative (one grandmother is dead, as are both grandfathers) to, in stanza two, darkly or sweetly suggestive (one aunt "went to the asylum," and the "7 yr old niece . . . is the only one that smiles at me"). The final two parentheticals, in the third stanza, are mostly concerned with the uncle "who disappeared when he was 15." It is part of the family mythology that the vanished uncle "just took / off and caught a freight." This is what "(they say)," at least. Among the nine other ancestors who "have the same name" as the speaker, it is this disappeared uncle who seems somehow to most resemble the speaker, at least in the terms of his absence. "He's discussed each year / when the family has a reunion"; he "causes uneasiness in / the clan, he is an empty space." Space is a critical word in this poem. It is the "space" of the speaker's cell the 47 faces "stare across," and "space" will return in the poem's final line. It is a grandmother who "keeps the Family Bible with everybody's birth dates," and then the final parenthetical in the first section—"(and death dates) in it."

Somehow, in the space between the speaker and his family, his incarceration is a kind of death unto itself, or a kind of near death; it is purgatorial, for sure. If there is no place in the grandmother's Bible "'for whereabouts unknown,'" in speaking of the gone uncle, there is also no place to note that the speaker with the same name is in prison.

Here's section 2:

Each Fall the graves of my grandfathers call me, the brown
hills and red gullies of mississippi send out their electric
messages, galvanizing my genes. Last yr/like a salmon quitting
the cold ocean—leaping and bucking up his birthstream/I
hitchhiked my way from L.A. with 16 caps in my pocket and a
monkey on my back. and I almost kicked it with the kinfolks.
I walked barefooted in my grandmother's backyard/I smelled
    the old

land and the woods/I sipped cornwhiskey from fruit jars
     with the men/
I flirted with the women/I had a ball til the caps ran out
and my habit came down. That night I looked at my
     grandmother
and split/my guts were screaming for junk/but I was almost
contented/I had almost caught up with me.
     (The next day in Memphis I cracked a croaker's crib for
     a fix.)

This yr there is a gray stone wall damming my stream,
     and when
the falling leaves stir my genes, I pace my cell or flop on
     my bunk
and stare at 47 black faces across the space. I am all of them,
they are all of me, I am me, they are thee, and I have no sons
to float in the space between.

The lines in the poem's second section get a little longer (in
the mass-market paperback-sized Hall, several do not fit on a single
line and have to be broken and indented); there are two stanzas of
thirteen and five lines respectively. Several times, in section two only,
Knight uses slashes mid-line. These are a propulsive and concentrating
strategy; they dramatize the effect of coming down, "til the caps ran
out." The first stanza is a narrative of what may have been the last
time the speaker was with his family, when "like a salmon quitting /
the cold ocean—leaping and bucking up his birthstream," he "almost
kicked it with the kinfolks." He'd hitchhiked from L.A. "with 16 caps
in my pocket and a / monkey on my back." It might have been one
of those family reunions spoken of in section one. He says "I walked
barefooted in my grandmother's backyard/I smelled the old / land
and the woods/I sipped corn whiskey from fruit jars with the men/ /
I flirted with the women." The habit is not kicked, however; it "came
down," and "[t]hat night I looked at my grandmother / and split."

This is that calm, that looking back from his cell, toward the gazes and the single smile of his kin. "[M]y guts," he says, "were screaming for junk/but I was almost / contented/I had almost caught up with me." That me is the person he was and now, distant and incarcerated, somehow is again, although now "there is a gray stone wall damming my stream," as the poem's final stanza begins. That "cold ocean" is a "gray stone" cell, and he returns to those "47 black faces across the space," a space now as small as his jail cell and as vast as the geography and the time and the sadness between them. Knight returns then to the phrasings of the end of section one: "I am all of them, / they are all of me, / I am me, they are thee," with this additional poignant and powerful difference: among all the forty-seven faces—parents, grandparents, brothers, sisters, uncles, aunts, cousins, nieces, and nephews—what is missing is a child of his own. Just as there is no child of his listed in the grandmother's Bible, there are pictures of "no sons" on that wall "to float in the space between." The space between, for now at least, is too large to be crossed but not to be imagined. The poem's much shorter final line suggests that space, and the speaker's absence.

In the summer of 1975, between my first and second years in graduate school, I traveled to Allendale, Michigan, to attend the third (and what would turn out to be the last) National Poetry Festival, at Grand Valley State Colleges. It was there I heard Etheridge Knight read "The Idea of Ancestry," and it was there I bought my copy of *Belly Song and Other Poems* ($1.75, one of the great bargains of my life). And it was there I had Knight sign the book for me. We talked a little. He was interested in the fact that I was born in East St. Louis; he had friends there, he said. We talked about Coltrane (I loved *Giant Steps*). When I told him I was a graduate student at Montana, he said, "Montana? Damn." I didn't ask what he meant by that. He inscribed the book "To Brother Bob Wrigley," and yes, I love that, though I understood then as I understand now that such a designation was a kindness he bestowed upon me. At best, we were brothers in the art, but if I was a poet, I was also a young and privileged white man.

And *Belly Song and Other Poems* is one of my most prized possessions. During the worst summers of wildfires here in Idaho, I go out to my little studio building and fill a box with books to keep in the garage for a quick getaway, books I don't think I can bear to lose. A couple of dozen usually. I have several thousand books out here, and hundreds of them are inscribed and signed, and for some reason I don't always pick the same ones. Except for *Belly Song and Other Poems*.

The wonderful thing about the National Poetry Festival, which was organized by the poet Robert Vas Dias, was how remarkably diverse it was (Vas Dias left Grand Valley State Colleges soon after the one I attended, and the festivals, sadly, ended with his departure). In 1975—in addition to Etheridge Knight—Nikki Giovanni, June Jordan, and Ishmael Reed were there. There were Asian poets: Filipino-, Japanese-, and Chinese-Americans: Mei-Mei Berssenbrugge, Jessica Hagedorn, Lawson Inada, Alex Kuo, and Shawn Wong. There were three Native American poets: Simon Ortiz, James Welch, and Leslie Silko. The white poets were Robert Bly, Robert Creeley, Galway Kinnell, James Wright, Ira Sadoff, Kathleen Fraser, and Diane Wakoski, among others. There were twenty-three featured poets at the National Poetry Festival in 1975, and more than half of them were poets of color. More than four decades ago.

Except for "The Idea of Ancestry," all the poems Knight read at the Festival in Allendale were from *Belly Song*. Its first printing, according to the copyright page, was "July, 1973," so it was just two years old. I'd already bought the book and was halfway reading along during his reading, although it proved very difficult not to keep my eyes on Knight. He read "Ilu, the Talking Drum"; he read "Dark Prophesy: I Sing of Shine"; he read "Belly Song." But the poem he read that hit me hardest, that astonished me most, was "Feeling Fucked/Up." Thirty-odd years ago, I taught it to a large class of freshmen lit students, in

Idaho (it is very likely those students were all white), and one of the students complained about it to my department chair (who told me to watch my fucking language). It made a few more uncomfortable, I'm sure. I don't know what they thought when I told them the poem was directly in the lineage of great lost/gone love poems in English, from the old anonymous "Western Wind," which I'd taught them a few weeks before, and in the lineage of the greatest songs of lost love; I don't know what they thought when I told them that in my opinion "Feeling Fucked/Up" was one of the greatest poems in the language. A few of them might have written that down in their notebooks.

I always imagine that Knight finished the poem then titled it. What else could it have been called?

> Lord she's gone done left me done packed/up
> 　　and split
> and i with no way to make her
> come back and everywhere the world is bare
> bright bone white crystal sand glistens
> dope death dead dying and jiving drove
> her away made her take her laughter and her smiles
> and her softness and her midnight sighs—
>
> Fuck Coltrane and music and clouds drifting in
> 　　the sky
> fuck the sea and trees and the sky and birds
> and alligators and all the animals that roam the earth
> fuck marx and mao fuck fidel and nkrumah and
> democracy and communism fuck smack and pot
> and red ripe tomatoes fuck joseph fuck mary fuck
> god jesus and all the disciples fuck fanon nixon
> and malcolm fuck the revolution fuck freedom fuck
> the whole muthafucking thing
> all i want now is my woman back
> so my soul can sing

The opening "Lord" makes the poem both a prayer and an apostasy, and it only gets worse for the deity. No doubt I feel some level of ordinary envy not of the speaker's irremediable loss but of the poet's profligate, relentless, and delicious use of one of the most forbidden words in the language (twelve fucks and one "muthafucking" in eleven lines of the second stanza; also the "fucked" in the title: fourteen in all, a little sonnet of fucks). I remember talking to that class full of freshmen about the word, about its power. Most of them had never heard it spoken in a classroom before, and a few of them—you could see it—were delighted not just to have heard it and heard it so many times but to have had the opportunity to say it in a classroom themselves (none of them had the slightest idea who "fanon" or "nkrumah" were). I've used the word in poems myself, but never with such abandon, and as one student put it, the poem loses all its power if you replace its fucks with damns, dangs, or durns.

But we also talked about the first stanza, in which there isn't fuck one. Actually, the poem *is* a kind of fourteen-lines-be-damned sonnet. The opening stanza is set-up, the situation, poetically and beautifully described; it functions the way the octave does in an Italian sonnet. And the second stanza, coming just after the turn toward meaning and fucked-uppedness, works like the sestet, in which everything a black man like Knight, in the last third of twentieth century America, might be most concerned with, including even "red ripe tomatoes" and "nixon," as well as "malcolm" and "the revolution." All fucked.

Among the many things that interest me in the poem is the function of figuration. Figures are clearly present in the opening stanza: "the world is bare / bright bone white." The lost love has taken away not only her literal "laughter" and "smiles" but her "softness" and "midnight sighs" as well, though I confess that I am not sure whether, in this context, they are examples of synecdoche or metonymy. Closely associated with or part of? Well, yeah, both.

But what about stanza two? Isn't everything from Coltrane (I love that this is the only capitalized proper noun in the poem, along, perhaps, with "Lord"), isn't everything, all the way to "freedom," in fact, metaphorical? Everything—"the whole muthafucking thing"—from the holiest musician of them all to "the sky and birds" is equally and summarily dismissed in the face of this loss, at least metaphorically. And the way the poem ends with an ABAB rhyming quatrain, in almost ever-diminishing lines, isn't that just genius? I think it is. When Knight read the poem that evening in Allendale, Michigan, he never even looked at the text. It was spoken. It felt spontaneous. And it felt absolutely honest and true. The rhyming of "the whole muthafucking thing" with "so my soul can sing" rang in that auditorium as pure, meaningful, and honest music.

"Feeling Fucked/Up" (the slash is present in the title in *Belly Song* but curiously not on the Poetry Foundation's website) is not in the Hall anthology; the poem may not have existed when Hall's revisions and enlargements were made (presumably in 1971 or '72). And maybe a poem called "Feeling Fucked/Up" might have pushed beyond the limits of some kind of respectability then, although Hall does include Ginsberg's "The End," which uses "fuckers" once (why not part one of "Howl," I wonder?). Of course, we know the poem isn't about the word "fuck"; the word is used only in its most decidedly negative sense, after all, and the absence of any positive associations has everything to do with the lover's absence. There may even be, now, well into the twenty-first century, certain aspects of male possession ("all I want now is *my* woman"—those are my italics) that might alienate some readers more than all the fucks.

The speaker's bereft by the loss of her, and nothing else matters but the way he feels, which is "fucked/up," so much so that his soul—the poem as evidence to the contrary notwithstanding—cannot sing. Knight's marriage to the poet Sonia Sanchez ended in 1970; it's hard to believe that Sanchez is not the woman in question. If art, as Edmund Wilson suggested, proceeds from a wound, the wound, in the case of both of these Etheridge Knight poems, is acknowledged as self-inflicted. What "Feeling Fucked/Up" captures is the moment when that wound is most fully acknowledged and remembered, and therefore felt. (A poem called "Being Fucked/Up" would be a completely other thing, wouldn't it?) It's a lyric poem; it captures that moment, which is a moment that can be relived both voluntarily and involuntarily. The speaker in "The Idea of Ancestry" sprawls on his bunk, with "no sons / to float in the space between." Otherwise, he abides. He waits for freedom and reunion, there being no other choice. In "Feeling Fucked/Up," the speaker longs only for the woman back, so his soul "can sing." That both poems manage, from the depths of their respective despairs, to be examples of the soul singing through poetry—singing in resolve and in agony, but singing nevertheless—is what has made me believe that Etheridge Knight is one of the truly great American poets of his century. His singular influence delights and inspires me.

It was a hard life. Knight died about six weeks before his sixtieth birthday, on March 10, 1991, in Indianapolis. I've visited his grave there. By the time he was the age I am today, he'd been dead for seven years.

THE MUSIC OF SENSE

Robert Frost didn't talk that much about his theories about writing poems. Opinionated, he was, but he was not the sort of poet inclined toward manifestoes. This is one of the things I suppose I admire most about him. His poems provide his example; his poetics are abundantly on display in the work itself. His occasional lectures—talks, really, casual and devoid of theoretical commentary—tend to be almost encoded, sly, and models of the very simple complexity his poems exemplify.

However, among those things he did say about the art, none is more telling, nor more useful for those of us who would write ourselves, than his ideas about what he called "the sound of sense." Frost believed that language, particularly syntax, is hard-wired within us. The sound of sense, according to Frost, was demonstrated in the fact that a conversation overheard on the other side of a wall, a conversation we are unable to discern the actual words of, carries within its sounds—its rhythms and inflections, its tonal modulations—what is at its most fundamental level *understandable*. Emotional and intellectual tenors are audible even though the individual words are not.

It's an interesting idea on a number of levels. For me, it has always suggested that it is possible, once a given rhythmical and musical context has been established in a poem, that a composing poet, in the very act of writing, might in fact *hear* the next line before it's put down; that the poet might not hear the words, but hears instead the shape of the words (through the wall, so to speak), and by that pre-written hearing, find a way into the poem's necessary statement, its fulfillment, even its meaning. And traditionally metrical as Frost's poems often are, I'm not talking about just fulfilling a final line of, say, iambic tetrameter. Frost was a consummate metrist, but a great metrist is not necessarily a great poet. Frost's iambic poems are full of initial trochees and terminal amphibrachs; he *substituted*, as we say, at will, and always for the best of effects. If he was not, as he famously suggested about free verse, interested in "playing tennis with the net down," he was also not inclined to keep lobbing the ball back and forth. He meant to hit a winner every time.

What I would like to suggest in this essay is either a refinement of Frost's "sound of sense," or an extrapolation from it. Maybe it's just that I'm not keen on his first term, "sound," which strikes me as inclusive but vague. When I talk about sound in poetry, I tend to use the more particular word "music." I believe language, both spoken and written, is inherently musical, and I believe that poetry is necessarily—not to mention historically, via its lyrical roots, its long-valued power as incantation—more closely aligned with musical notation. All written and spoken language has rhythm, but poetry, even the most liberated of free verse, must use rhythm in the service of the poem's larger aims. And strung across the poem's rhythmical order, the very sounds the words make—the bells and calls of the vowels, the percussion of the consonants—create, in the best poems, a rhetorical apparatus that is, or that must aspire to, the condition of music.

(This is not, I don't think, an aspiration solely of poetry either. The best prose is equally aware of and continually working toward the same musical condition. When we talk about a writer's "prose style," we are, I think, talking about the way she or he approaches the musical composition of syntax. Fundamentally, every sort of spoken or written eloquence is, at the level I'm speaking of, musical.)

Frost's other term, "sense," I am very fond of. It's a much richer term, to be sure. I love the idea that a poet's primary occupation may be the *making* of sense, both as a kind of deep, even bottomless, rightness, and also as a direct appeal to the body, the brain's elaborate sensory apparatus. The making of sense requires, in other words, not only apprehensibility (and, yes, comprehensibility: the poem must be, at some level, after some measure of readerly endeavor, somehow fathomable, or maybe enterable), but the poem must also be possessed of a bodily connection as well (feelable, you might say). The senses are how we *make sense* of what we think and imagine and come to know. Music—pure music, played on instruments or sung by human voices—engages our auditory sense first, but we all know that music extends itself into our other senses as well. We feel music as well as hear it. We see its effect on us. Poetry works the same way. Most of us come to a poem on the page in order to know *what* it will tell us. But the music of its delivery—*how* it makes its case—is not only inseparable from what it says, it is a central component of the poem's content. It is the senses' contribution to the poem's larger intellectual and emotional sense.

I'm going to talk about a poem that demonstrates what I mean. It's by Richard Hugo. It's called "Trout":

> Quick and yet he moves like silt.
> I envy dreams that see his curving
> silver in the weeds. When stiff as snags
> he blends with certain stones.
> When evening pulls the ceiling tight
> across his back he leaps for bugs.
>
> I wedged hard water to validate his skin—
> call it chrome, say red is on
> his side like apples in a fog, gold
> gills. Swirls always looked one way
> until he carved the water into many
> kinds of current with his nerve-edged nose.
>
> And I have stared at steelhead teeth
> to know him, savage in his sea-run growth,
> to drug his facts, catalog his fins
> with wings and arms, to bleach the black
> back of the first I saw and frame the cries
> that sent him snaking to oblivions of cress.

I don't think you have to be a trout fisher to understand this poem, but it doesn't hurt. Hugo was and I am, but I don't think my love of trout fishing has much more than a minimal effect on my reading of this poem. Though it's called "Trout," and though it is, at the surface, a poem *about* trout, it is also—as is nearly every other literary document composed in the first person—very much about its speaker, that "I" who appears four times just in the poem's three stanzas. I'll come back to this point at my conclusion, but for now I'll simply say this: Hugo was a student of the great Theodore Roethke, and while Roethke is not universally referred to as a "Confessional poet," his primary subject through much of his career was simply his struggle with the self, with the fact and illusion of identity. Over the decades of his writing life, Roethke devised a way of transferring his emotional struggles into his descriptions of natural landscapes. (His late meditations, such as the "North American Sequence," are *tours de force* performances in this regard.) Though Hugo outgrew, or moved away from, this particular Roethkean approach, this is an early Hugo poem, and Roethke's touch is easily seen on it.

It is the music of the poem that sets out its particular tone. From the first line, the poem is an act of mythologizing. The trout is, after all, just a fish, even as the poem makes it clearly something much larger and more significant. Listen to the first line: "Quick and yet he moves like silt." Like most of the rest of the poem, this line is composed in a very tightly controlled tetrameter. All seven words are monosyllables and the meter is absolutely syncopated: QUICK and YET he MOVES like SILT. What's interesting to me is less the regular rhythm, however, as what we might call the duration of the stressed words here. If you've ever watched a trout in a stream, then you can see that this description is among the most accurate ever written. The startled trout, or the hunting fish, is exceptionally "quick" indeed, and it is the sound (yes, the music) of the first two stressed words in the line that duplicates the trout's great quickness. It's the Q, the hard K, and the T sounds, in part. They tick quickly off the tongue. But it's also the vowels, that short I and short E, that make the words themselves quick-moving. They spend very little time being said. Conversely, the end of the line, the third and fourth stressed syllables, stretch out and elongate. It's the labial M, and V, the Ss, and the L, and it's the long-U sound of the O in move. It's not really possible to make these sounds quickly. The line slows as the fish slows. I love the fact that the subject of the sentence, the "he," the fish itself, is smack in the middle of the line, three pertinent words on either side, a kind of fulcrum that moves us from the fleet "quick and yet" to the dawdling "moves like silt." Even the fact that Hugo ends this first line as a clipped single sentence is part of his strategy: it's dramatic, a kind of declaration that demands elaboration.

Interestingly, that elaboration, when it comes in the next sentence, brings with it the speaker himself. Again, line two is straight iambic tetrameter, with an amphibrach—an extra unstressed syllable—in the fourth position. He's managing to be both highly traditional, metrically, and yet he's also able to riff, so to speak, inside that tradition: the first tetrameter line's a syllable short; the second's a syllable long.

But notice the music in the sentence that makes up line two and half of line three: there are four long E sounds in the sentence; five, in a way, since that –i-n-g at the end of "curving" echoes the same sound in the line's context. I'm going to argue that this is a primal kind of music. There's something entirely bodily and spontaneous in the long E sound, something halfway delirious and charged with excitement (it's why we say Whee! on the rollercoaster and not k-k-k-k-k); it's a sound you can make with a smile. And after all, the word that starts this chain of long E sounds is the word "envy." It's a curious word, at this point in the poem, and one that can be challenging too. That is, exactly what does the speaker in the poem envy? Well, he envies dreams that see. Trout are hard to see in the water; sometimes you can be looking right at one and not see it, especially if it's "in the weeds."

Sometimes the fish is there then not then there again; the trout in its element is ideal, and the one who sees the trout is lucky, careful, discerning. In a sense, the speaker's envying a kind of clarity that only occurs in dreams. Or in poems.

Line three's also tetrameter, with nine syllables, only this time the substitution's yet a third alternative: line one, a missing unstressed syllable at the beginning of the line; line two, an additional unstressed syllable at the end of the line; and line three, an additional stressed syllable at the beginning of the line. If line two (and half of three) are pumped up tonally with the exuberance of the long E (and that excitable envy), then the second half of line three and all of line four are just the opposite, with the quiet hisses of soft Cs and Ss, and the similarly-made Ns—do a quick census of Ss and Ns here; it's pretty startling how many there are in such a short sentence. (Note too, the shortness of line 4: this is a tetrameter poem and here's an absolutely lock-step iambic line, only it's just three feet long. Hugo's still not given us a perfectly regular tetrameter line. This is no accident. We're off-balance and carefully concentrating, almost as though we were standing in a swift-moving stream.)

The stanza's fourth sentence is its longest and its most interesting, I think. Line five is—finally—the first impeccable iambic tetrameter line. Line six is the second. But even here, his manipulation of the lines within the sentence's construction camouflage the meter. There's a good reason—despite the fact that this sentence is a complex one, with clear subordinate and main clauses—that Hugo doesn't use a comma in it: I mean, which is it? Does evening pull the ceiling tight across the trout's back? Or does the trout leap "across his back" for bugs? It's both, of course. What Hugo's done here, with a line break and the strategic omission of a comma, is to reinforce the main idea of this entire stanza: he's quick and slow, he's curving and stone, he's there and not there at all.

And one more thing: notice how this first stanza's rhymes

function for the same reason: silt/tight; curving/stone; snags/bugs: they're there, but they sort of aren't there too. In this poem, Hugo's a poet who's possessed of what I'll call 360-degree peripheral vision: he's seeing all his effects simultaneously and deploying them all for the poem's single effect.

In the rhyme department, note that the first two lines of stanza two, employ exactly the same sort of rhyme strategy all of stanza one features—but after that, no rhymes at all in stanza two. Or are there?

The point is, Hugo never stops considering all the musical possibilities—meter, assonance, alliteration, and rhyme—and he wields them with considerable effectiveness over the grid of lines and syntax.

Things change somewhat in stanza two. The speaker makes his second appearance in the first word, but we don't spend a lot of time thinking about him. He's there throughout, but there's only that one first person pronoun and the implied "to me" that comes in line four ("swirls always looked" [to me]). But another reason the "I" recedes is that the diction forces a kind of distance. Many readers, for instance, are puzzled by the first verb, "wedged." What on earth does that mean? they wonder. It's a semi-visual image, really; a conceptual figure. We're talking moving water here, "hard water," mountain water, the sort preferred by trout everywhere. Stand in such a stream, and you become a wedge in the water, dividing a single motion into two. This is important to the poem's ultimate meaning, this wedging. If in stanza one, the speaker envies the trout's motions, here it is his own diametrically opposite sort of motion featured. There's no there-and-not-there for the speaker. He's not IN his element, but he's there to "validate" the trout's skin. *Validate?* Validate is such an ugly, unpoetic word, really (although, having three syllables, the first and third stressed, it slips very nicely into any sort of iambic construction), but that's the point, that seeming ugliness: the tone at the beginning of this stanza implies a kind of desperate yearning, an enormous need to see and experience the trout's perfection in its own element.

It's interesting to me that, following that odd word "validate," there are a couple of lines of almost rhapsodic poetic language: "call it chrome, say red is on / his side like apples in a fog, gold / gills." Notice how line three's got four successive iambs, then an odd stressed word from the next syntactical unit attached to it—that "gold" in "gold gills." Why? Two reasons, I think: first, there's the long O sound in gold he's going to pick up in "nose" three lines later; and second, Hugo loved the idea of "gills" coming right next to "swirls," as though the very part of the fish that allows it to live in the water is as illusive as the water's swirls—not to mention, he probably just liked how gills and swirls look together.

Line four is a metrical bass drum: there are seven syllables in the line, and by my count the only one unstressed is the second syllable in "always." The effect of this is hard to hear, or see, I think. There's a way in which all those stresses take the poem to its metrical crisis: as nearly all the rest of the poem is iambically syncopated, this line is where the desperation gets the best of the speaker. Drawn by the "apples in a fog," by those "gold / gills," the speaker's very vision of the fish *is* a kind of validation, but only of the trout, not of himself, and it's his own validation he seeks, his own worthiness. Listen to the last two lines of stanza two: "until he carved the water into many / kinds of current with his nerve-edge nose." Line five is iambic with a terminal amphibrach; the meter established in that line forces us to read line six as a continuation of it, the effect of which is to turn the meter around, from iambic to trochaic, and ending with three hard-stressed syllables. And the fact is, there's no more rhythmical passage in the poem. You can almost rap these lines; they're imposingly, masterfully metered.

The speaker's presence in stanza three is more centered here, for this stanza is the poem's summation. If he envied the trout its perfection in stanza one, and if he sought to see and know that perfection in stanza two, what happens in stanza three is conclusion, and is, alas, failure, at least at the level of the speaker's quest. He *has* known this fish. He's stared at the steelhead's teeth "to know him." He's attempted to "drug his facts," to make the facts of the fish something that will speak to him of his own life, his own experience and potential. He's meant to "catalog his fins / with wings and arms": yes, the fish's fins are kind of like wings, but a whole lot less like arms. I admit, these verbs are challenging, chosen, I believe, as "validate" was, for their human ham-handedness. Of these, "bleach" may be most challenging, though I believe he's aiming with that verb to pull from the black mystery of the trout's "black back" some sense of his own validation.

The hope, the aspiration, the point of it all, is simply this: That he—the speaker—might be, somehow, as perfectly suited to his own world as the trout is to his.

But it's not to be. The last two lines are remembrance: imagine the young Richard Hugo, wading the streams of his native western Washington, and seeing the fish—in the way he has made clear that one *does* see trout; it's always surprising—and this one's huge, a returning-to-spawn bull steelhead, probably as long as the speaker's leg. What does he do? He screams, and the trout vanishes, "snaking to oblivions of cress." Even the fact that Hugo chooses to make oblivion plural—oblivions!—is part of his musical strategy. That S ties the *idea* of oblivion to cress, to cries, and to sent and snaking. Above all there's "oblivion," coming from the Latin, and meaning simply a state of forgottenness. There's something going on here, some deeper complexity emerging. Indeed, the trout may well be perfectly suited to its world in a way no human being ever is to his or her own; on the other hand, this human construction, this poem, is itself a trout; certainly it is called "Trout"—and if there is any justice, the human, the poet, might just avoid the oblivion that the trout, in its perfection, can both never escape and has no need to fear.

Note too, how the rhyme, like that trout in the moving water, has returned: there in lines one and two, with teeth/growth; then gone with fins/black; then back with cries/cress. All of these musical effects are in the service of the poem's—go ahead, say it—MEANING.

And I need to say this: at one level, the poem is indeed no more than a tribute to a beautiful aquatic animal, one that the poet reveres, and I suppose one is lucky if one also reveres the trout, in coming to love this poem. But if that were all it is—if all the poem aimed to do was pay homage to the trout via a dead-on description—then there'd be no reason for the speaker's presence. The poem's about the speaker. The poem sets up its juxtaposition between the trout and the seeking, envying, validating, cataloging man—the main character, the poet. And the trout, in some ways, emerges vastly superior, though I would argue that the poet, the poet who wields all the powers of language as well as the trout wields its body in water, comes as close to perfection as it is possible to come. As for the man, well, they're not so different after all. In the end, equally anonymous, each one is bound for his own oblivion.

There's yet a bit more though. When I brought up Roethke some pages ago, particularly Roethke's transference of his emotional and psychic states into and onto the landscape itself, I meant that you should understand this poem of Hugo's as a similar endeavor. That is, there are things about Hugo's life you will know if you've read his poems very carefully, or perhaps if you've read his prose—most especially the autobiographical essays in *The Triggering Town* and the whole of his posthumous, cobbled-together and yet still wonderful autobiography, *The Real West Marginal Way*. I'm going to tell you a few things now, not because they are necessary to your understanding of "Trout," but because, now that you've been led through the poem, these "facts" of Hugo's life might well make the poem even richer.

"Trout" is the first poem in Hugo's *Collected Poems*, the first in his *Selected*, and in his first book, *A Run of Jacks*. It is, in other words, not only an early poem, but a seminal one. He was fresh from his studies at the University of Washington, from his work with Theodore Roethke, and Roethke's influence is apparent not so much in the way Hugo arrays and deploys his poetic effects as in the poem's deeply buried central, and very personal, concern. In Roethke's case that meant the landscapes he confronted were primal, sexual, and deeply, if slantedly, revealing.

In the case of Hugo's poem, the landscape and the trout of the title are a reflection of Hugo's own long, difficult, and often painful discovery of himself. Abandoned by his young mother, Hugo was raised by cold, distant, and sometimes cruel maternal grandparents (he was, he said, subjected now and then to "gratuitous beatings"). His name at birth was not Hugo, but Hogan. Richard F. Hogan. It was after his mother married Mr. Hugo that Dick changed his name. Perhaps he thought that might reingratiate him to his mother, but she never reclaimed him, and much of his life, for reasons too complex to attempt to analyze here but central to his endeavors as a poet, he felt himself to be "a wrong thing in a right world."

The trout, most especially the steelhead at the end of the poem is, like all wild animals, utterly at home in its own skin, absolutely suited to the world it lives in, a very right thing in a clearly right world. When the speaker, in memory, cries out on seeing his first steelhead and thereby sends it "snaking to oblivions of cress," that moment is transcendent, though it is also sadly validating. Everything the trout is, from its majesty to its ease within itself, is what the speaker is not.

Much of Hugo's life was marred by his childhood. He did not trust the idea of love. His relations with women were soured for decades. He felt himself to be inherently unlovable. And you can find a lot of this sort of thing—rarely in the form of self-pity or woeful whininess—in his poems. And though he did, to a large part, write himself well, or manage to write himself past such a childhood, he also understood, late in his life, as he struggled to early on, that his childhood was his master narrative, a story he would have to grapple with and come to an understanding of, then work to revise.

It's really no different for any of us; everyone's got a master narrative. Hugo's challenge was to mold that narrative to an art that was welcoming and moving. I believe "Trout," this early and seminal poem, makes everything that came after in Hugo's writing life possible. Among his many bromides regarding poetry, perhaps Hugo's most famous assertion is this, and I have to say it is the one I've carried with me most consciously for the last three-and-a-half decades. He said, "if you have to make a choice between music and meaning, pick music every time." Take care of the music of the language; concentrate less on what you're saying than on how you get it said; and meaning—believe it or not—will take care of itself. And if you've lived up to that sort of directive, you might well write something more than a poem. You might write a living example of poetry. An imaginary river with a real trout in it.

This is the only thing worth aspiring to as a poet.

ON THE STREET WHERE YOU LIVE

"Love takes time to overcome."—Confucius

Certain love songs beloved by men are listened to with something like derision by women. So I have been assured, by a woman, and I wonder about that. I don't doubt it, but I wonder. I have known for many years that most of the canonical American songbook "torch songs," for example, were written by men but in their classic versions sung by women. The woman would never get over the loss of the man for whom she carried forever "a torch." Right.

But I would like to consider a song almost diametrically the opposite of a torch song. I mean "On the Street Where You Live," jaunty and upbeat, its lyrics by Alan Jay Lerner, from the musical play *My Fair Lady* (Frederick Loewe wrote the music), first staged in 1956, when I was five. The film version, which I saw in a theater in St. Louis with my parents and sister, appeared in 1964, right about the time I crashed face-first into puberty. I remember being resistant to the improbable fact that the handsome young Englishman was standing on the street and singing, with orchestral accompaniment, but I also remember thinking that such a feeling as he expressed (turns out the actor was lip-synching; someone else did the expressing), that that feeling might be—I didn't know—*real*. I suppose I wanted it to be. Why wouldn't I? He seemed so happy, so thrilled, that young man, and the lyrics of the song represented his happiness very convincingly, even to, or perhaps especially to, a thirteen year old boy.

Somehow, I'm sixty-eight now, a year older than Alan Jay Lerner was when he died in 1986 of lung cancer, impoverished, owing the IRS over a million dollars, and unable to pay his medical bills. Lerner was married eight times. He said once, "All I can say is if I had no flair for marriage, I also had no flair for bachelorhood." (Something in that quip and its delivery is in his best lyrics too.) It seems that Mr.

Lerner might have felt the exhilaration his song expresses a few more times than anyone ought to.

The character who sings the song in *My Fair Lady*, one Freddy Eynsford-Hill, is lost in infatuation with Eliza Doolittle, the Cockney flower girl taken in by Professor Henry Higgins, after she comes to him seeking elocution lessons. (The play, of course, is adapted from George Bernard Shaw's *Pygmalion*.) Professor Higgins wagers with his friend and houseguest, Colonel Pickering, that he can turn Eliza into a passable young "lady," one who can, with his lessons, function in the upper social caste of which he and Pickering are a part.

The scene in which Freddy falls for Eliza takes place at a gathering of exceeding privilege and decorousness, at a race track. Women in gowns and elaborate, even outlandish, hats; men in top hats, tails, and spats. The musical number in the scene is "Ascot Gavotte" (also known as "Ascot Opening Day"—its opening lines: "Ev'ry duke and earl and peer is here/Ev'ryone who should be here is here"). Eliza does quite well among the hoity-toity until, in the midst of the race's final stretch she can stand it no longer and with all her suppressed Cockney fervor bellows at her favored horse, "Come on, Dover! Move yer bloomin' arse!" The vocal intro to "On the Street Where You Live" includes Freddy remembering, and repeating, Eliza's unfortunate (or fortunate) ejaculation; it even suggests that that ejaculation may be what, beyond Eliza herself (played in the film by Audrey Hepburn), precipitates his headlong fall.

Soon thereafter Freddy arrives at Professor Higgins's house with flowers. Higgins, Pickering, and Eliza are having dinner. The maid takes the flowers and invites Mr. Eynsford-Hill in, but he declines and at the bottom of the stair, back on the street, sings his song.

The plays, both the musical and its Shavian model, are fraught. Shaw took as his inspiration an ancient Greek myth. Pygmalion was a sculptor who fell in love with one of his statues, which—presumably so deeply and intimately loved and, much more importantly, so perfectly created—comes to life. In Lerner and Loewe's version, Eliza is matter, medium, raw material fashioned by a man into an acceptable, respectable, lovable, and cravable woman—made so, created even, by a man.

To say that the gender issues in the movie went right over my head at thirteen is accurate and predictable and an understatement. Although one might also say that the issues went over a lot of heads: both the plays and the film were enormously successful.

But Freddy seems head over heels for a fully-formed woman, as far as he can tell, one who is just enough like but not at all like the other women in his circle. Something about class is involved in it too, of course; Eliza's sudden coarseness is electrifying. Who knows what it might suggest to Freddy? But what I'm curious about is this: could "On the Street Where You Live" be one of those love songs beloved by men but derided by women? Does the man's infatuation seem, well, fatuous? The word "love" is never spoken in the song. Does infatuation really have anything to do with love? (One might ask the same thing about music or poetry.) Freddy has seen but hardly even met Eliza—just once—but he is intoxicated by her, the possibility of her. He's smitten. Is it Freddy's smittenness itself that is suspect? Is the very act of feeling smitten by another person suspect? In the hetero-world, in and out of movies, it's usually the man who is smote, so to speak, and his condition, in terms literary and historical—and in reality—is all too often dangerous for the woman. Think of Daphne and Apollo, Zeus and Leda. The list is endless; it is added to every day in brutal stories in the news. Vastly more women are killed by obsessed lovers and husbands than by infatuated strangers.

Is Freddy's smittenness a form of potentially dangerous, power-mad insanity? Probably not. He seems too callow to be a monster. Shaw resisted the "happy ending," with Eliza and Higgins in love and together; the musical, not so much. Higgins seems to realize his love, or his loss (though of what, exactly? His dejected song, "I've Grown Accustomed to Her Face," is another of the musical's long-lived chestnuts). But then Eliza returns. The happy ending is at least implied. As for Freddy, when Eliza leaves Higgins earlier, she tells him she'll marry Freddy because he, at least, is one who loves her. But in the end, that doesn't matter. She comes back to the man who, as it were, made her what she is.

Are song lyrics poetry? Are they literature? The Nobel Committee says they are, and it's true that most of Bob Dylan's songs are vastly more literary than those of Alan Jay Lerner. By comparison, most of Lerner's songs are confections. On the page, "On the Street Where You Live" fluffs like meringue next to "Subterranean Homesick Blues." Then again, on the page, "Subterranean Homesick Blues" looks a little loose, compared to "The Waste Land." Then again once more, neither "Subterranean Homesick Blues" nor "The Waste Land" concerns itself with love, neither as a suspicious trope nor as an intense and possibly beautiful madness. (This might be the point at which to suggest the reader take a look at the lyrics to Dylan's "Lay Lady Lay." Love poems, love songs. It seems they all do what it is they always do.)

Love poems themselves don't usually seem to be after something more, or other, than love, the feeling of it, the joy or wretchedness that accompanies it. Not even Donne's "The Sun Rising" seems interested in the building of some sort of significant cultural edifice (I almost used "erection" instead of "building" but thought better of it; WWJD?).

The world of song, however, is still dominated by, one could even say drowned in, the subject of love. Love gone wrong, love lost, love in the midst of its lavishness. Schlock and corniness and worse abound. Then again, there's a lot to say about love. Isn't there? (I was in a rock band in high school, a cover band, and it is with no little shame and great reluctance that I confess to you that we learned to play, and actually performed, at least once or twice, "Yummy, Yummy, Yummy, I Got Love in My Tummy.") One of my favorite old jokes goes like this: A piano man in a bar plays a song so beautiful that everyone in the place is practically in tears. Someone asks, who wrote that song?

Piano man responds that he did, but that no one's ever been interested in recording or publishing it. The patrons are shocked. I call it, says the piano man, "I Love You So Fucking Much I Could Shit."

But what about "On the Street Where You Live"? Read it on the page and it automatically loses an edge, maybe its best edge. This is the nature of popular songs, of course. Or possibly it is the nature of all songs.

How close is "On the Street Where You Live" to poetry? Is such a measurement useful or even possible? My assumption has always been that Lerner wrote the lyrics first, knowing the situation (the book) and the narrative of the play, then Loewe set the words to music.

Here's the first verse:

> I have often walked down this street before,
> But the pavement always stayed beneath my feet before.
> All at once am I several stories high,
> Knowing I'm on the street where you live.

The opening line, divided midway by an unpunctuated caesura, is almost perfectly syncopated between stressed and unstressed syllables. Ten syllables, all the odd-numbered ones stressed. Line two *is* perfectly syncopated, but thirteen syllables long, with a double, almost identical, rhyme—"street before" / "feet before." Line three is the most interesting to me, simply because it contains its own rhyme: "all at once am I several stories high." And yet, as with line one, it's ten syllables in exactly the same meter as line one, with an identical unpunctuated caesura. The presence of that in-line rhyme manages to disguise the fact that line four rhymes with nothing, except perhaps itself, as the final phrase, the song's title, the refrain at the end of each verse. And interestingly, line four, though it is similarly syncopated as the other lines, has a trimeter feel. It is, in fact, a line of three cretic feet (stressed–unstressed–stressed) in nine syllables.

Verse two:

> Are there lilac trees in the heart of town?
> Can you hear a lark in any other part of town?
> Does enchantment pour out of every door?
> No, it's just on the street where you live.

The meter's identical to verse one. Maybe this is Lerner's musical knowledge at work. Loewe might have appreciated the metrical unity. Three questions metrically identical to three declarative statements; that's nice. Is that almost an in-line rhyme (lark/part) in line two? The in-line rhyme of the third line is in place again, as in the first verse, and metrically it *has to be* "No, it's just," to begin the final line; imagine the composer's chagrin (not to mention the singer's) if the meter were inside out and it read "It's only …." There is surely something valuable, even treasured, in a lyric's singability. The final line is, again, composed of three cretic feet.

The bridge, altered by the melody, is also altered by meter.

Bridge:

> And, oh, the towering feeling,
> Just to know somehow you are near.
> The overpowering feeling
> That any second you may suddenly appear.

The first three lines are shortened to eight syllables, lines one and three with a pyhrric foot (two syllables, neither stressed) in the third position. The fourth line is twelve syllables, six iambs, the first, the only, strictly iambic line in the song.

Something about the bridge also makes it the weightiest passage in the lyric. The towering, overpowering feeling may be the closest the song gets to a central issue and aspect of love. Then again, maybe not.

It may be the imagined dream of love through the eyes, or the heart, of the one who is, at this point, no more than infatuated.

Final verse:

> People stop and stare, they don't bother me,
> For there's nowhere else on earth that I would rather be.
> Let the time go by, I don't care if I
> Can be here on the street where you live.

Back to the beginning all over. Ten almost syncopated syllables, a punctuated caesura this time. Another thirteen syllables, syncopated, in line two (if you insist on stressing "there's" you complicate the stress of the first syllable in "nowhere," which, sorry, would be tin-eared and barbaric). Line three: internal rhyme, same meter as all other lines one and three. The most interesting thing is way *this* line three ends with the subject of the familiar clause that is line four. It might seem poetically a radical enjambment, but it facilitates the meter of the final near-refrain line and the internal rhyme. It also employs the same long-I rhyme as line three in the first verse, in which the subject is the first person pronoun, both the speaker/singer and the poem's true concern. Line four: three cretic feet yet again.

That's all, folks.

This precision, if that's what it is (or dogged metrical regularity?), of the lyric's form, verse after verse, including the bridge, is what pleases and delights me, and that delight is something I feel reading the lyric on the page. However, even if I read the verses aloud, I still hear them being sung in my mind's ear. I wonder if that metrical precision, or that mechanical sameness, is too much for poetry but exactly what is necessary in a song.

Wait, though. Is it still, somehow, a poem? Or rather, is it—can it possibly be—poetry? Probably not, though it is a song lyric of im-

153

pressive achievement, if not a lot of intellectual or even emotional heft. Part of the pleasure of it is wit—syntactical wit, rhyme wit, metrical wit; wit at the level of musical enactment; wit expressed as a mode of sweetness, rather than as something sharper or darker. There's nothing at all ironic about these lyrics. Well, maybe the people who stop and stare, as if it were some sort of meta-commentary on the bizarre existence of musical theater and film.

It's worth noting that, in poetic terms, the poem's an apostrophe. It's spoken to someone not-there as though she were. Freddy's Eliza as Petrarch's Laura. Sometimes, in the world of poetry, and of song, as in the world itself, one meets—or does not meet but merely sees—another person and is something like thunderstruck. Or to use a word I confess I am especially fond of, gobsmacked. Most often the thunderstruck or gobsmacked one does not bring flowers and walk along the street singing, nor does he write 366 sonnets to/about/for his never-to-be requited love and its object. If you were a woman whose appearance or passing acquaintance provoked singing in the street or hundreds of sonnets—enough to build an immortal career around (not to mention one of the most enduring verse forms in literary history)—might you, nevertheless, feel uneasy? Even stalked, in some way? Harassed or menaced? Maybe. (I don't think anyone ever asked Laura.) "On the Street Where You Live" may not be a love song at all, but a sub-species of the love song, which might be what would make some women, or even men, deride it. It's about fixation, obsession; and it speaks not at all of the target of that fixation and what such an obsession might feel like to her.

Does this kind of enchantment, or smittenness, the fact of thunderstruckness, actually happen? Sure. Does it happen to women, so that women feel it for men? I believe it surely does. Is it as potentially dangerous for the man who is the object of it (we've all seen *Fatal Attraction*)? Of course not. Are love songs more significant culturally than love poems? Almost certainly. More artful? No.

It may simply be that poems are poems and songs are songs. Love songs are not love poems but love songs. And still, according to the Nobel Committee, songs are literature.

Neither, I might say in response, are all poems.

"On the Street Where You Live" has been recorded hundreds of times, by (to name just a few) Shirley Horn, Nat King Cole, Peggy Lee, Rickie Lee Jones, Nancy Wilson, and Marvin Gaye. Great performers all and, as the short list here shows, as many women singers as men. (We presume male singers of many love songs, probably mistakenly. It intrigues me that Ella Fitzgerald, Karrin Allyson, Ernestine Anderson, Shirley Bassey, Chris Connor, and Dee Dee Bridgewater, among many other women, have recorded "Angel Eyes." Why should we have a harder time imagining a woman singing "Drink up, all you people?") Is a woman's infatuation with a man more difficult to imagine or to accept?

"On the Street Where You Live" is a good song, but if you take it away from its melody, it falls out of delightfulness into something clever, very well-composed lyrically, even deft, but almost ordinary, if there is an ordinary way to say *I am gobsmacked*. I have heard a number of musical renditions of Byron's "She Walks In Beauty," and none of them has been nearly as pleasing to my ear as Nat King Cole singing "On the Street Where You Live."

Byron's poem is better without music. Can anyone name a song lyric that is better without its music?

It was a 1992 recording of "On the Street Where You Live" by Harry Connick, Jr., I heard on the local jazz station a month or so ago. I was driving, alone. I'm sure I've heard many other versions of the song in the fifty-five years since I was thirteen, with my parents and sister in the St. Louis theater, but something about this particular rendition made me hear the song a little differently, or a little more clearly. Maybe it was the minimal accompaniment. There's no orchestra, no band, no combo, just Connick, Jr., on the piano and singing.

Nothing special about the piano work, finally. He's a very fine pianist, but not a great player. And Connick's singing clearly riffs on Sinatra, the latter's phrasing and tonal modulations. But for some reason I found myself engrossed in the lyrics, in the meter and rhyme, in the formal components that make song lyrics so much *like* poetry. When I got home, I looked up the song on the internet, printed off the lyrics, scanned them, and made notes. I actively—although it's not an especially demanding text—studied the meter of those lyrics.

What was I after? I knew it wasn't poetry before I started. Didn't I? Still, I want to say that I know the feeling the song expresses, I'm sure of it. I have felt it, I'm absolutely certain. I remember it well. But I don't know, or don't know anymore, if it is, or was, real, or how it might have been, or what it meant, if it were real. Or if it mattered, or mattered to anybody else. But I remember the feeling as extraordinary. To me. Or did I merely import Freddy Eynsford-Hill's gassed up idea of it when I was thirteen? It might be that this is the thing about certain love songs some women might recognize. And mistrust, at least.

They're all about Freddy, or the Dylan of "Lay Lady Lay." Or Alan Jay Lerner, or me.

WHAT THE RIVER SAYS

" . . . that is what I say." –William Stafford

If you were a salmon and had made your way for a couple of years in the Pacific, and had eluded predators and gill nets and passed by several thousand brightly colored lures and flies and baited hooks, and had managed, by dint of power and tirelessness, according to some spark of memory or instinct, to get up the ladders and around the nine dams on the Columbia and the Lower Snake, and past the last slackwater reservoir at Lewiston, Idaho, you might arrive here finally, where I am, at the bottom end of Hells Canyon, at the mouth of your namesake stream. You might be here, though few of your kind make it this far, and most that do are hatchery fish, still rugged and strong, but spawned at fish factories like the ones at Rapid River, near Riggins, or farther upstream, across the state, at Stanley Basin.

If, on the other hand, you were a wild fish, you might exhibit something a little like relief here, a little like joy or even love; no one knows, you might actually sense the very pebbles you were born out of. You might hole up in these deep pools at the confluence of your river and the Snake; you might roll and bask, rest up for a while, luxuriate in the odd primordial knowledge of your original water, then head off, upstream again, through the many rapids—Eye of the Needle, Snow Hole, China Bar, Elkhorn, Big Mallard, Salmon Falls—all the way to the river's headwaters at Galena and up a side creek there, to a bed of sand and pea gravel, where you'd deposit your eggs in a redd you sculpted with your tail, or, if you were a male, where you'd spread your milt over that same redd, fertilizing the eggs of the mate whose laying you stood guard to, and who, like you, will soon be dead and fed on by a bear or a clutch of lucky ravens. By anyone's measure, your journey is heroic, difficult in times immemorial, before dams and fisheries, before sonar and monofilament and high-tech tackle, before dewatering from irrigation and runoff of herbicides and the noxious spill from feedlots and ranches raising cattle and sheep. Your scarcity in the river named for you—wild salmon, you are—is one of North America's greatest environmental shames. And the source of it all, this still-beautiful river, clear and cold, a river made of many forks and tributary streams, what shall we call it when you are all gone, you survivors, you throwback anachronisms, you apparently doomed, romantic symbols of human folly and contempt? When that day comes, if it comes, the river will be a monument, a tombstone, a cenotaph, and what joy we take in its beauty, its rapids, its postcard scenery, will be tempered by the elegy of its name.

I have set foot in or floated over or looked upon many miles of the Salmon River and its tributaries. I have fished for trout on the East Fork of the South Fork and on the Secesh. I have picked perfect pie cherries at the old homestead near Wind River pack bridge. I have camped at Bear Lake, in Cougar Basin, and known that the spill from the lake will eventually flow past this spot at the Salmon's mouth. I have hunted chukar on the breaks above Riggins and visited with Sylvan Hart, better known as Buckskin Billy, the "Last of the Mountain Men," at Five Mile Bar on the Main Salmon, the actual "River of No Return."

But that part of the river I know best, and, by my knowing, love most, is the fifty-two miles or so from where I am today—leaned against a rock hot from the sun, at the confluence of the Salmon with the Snake—upstream to White Bird Creek. The Lower Salmon, this stretch is called. It's the bottom of the whole, nowhere-dammed, entirely free-flowing river system. It can be reached by gravel road from the Idaho side at three places—Hammer Creek, Graves Creek, and Eagle Creek—but the best way to see it, to know it, is by boat, a float boat—raft, kayak, drift boat—*downstream*, the direction in which it is first known by the salmon fry hatched along its reaches, the way it is encoded in them: a source, somewhere to come home to.

I have learned, over the last three decades and more, a few things about this stretch of river: where the remnants of Chinese rock houses can be found, primitive but sturdy shelters where former railroad workers holed up away from the white racist towns to mine a little gold and get by; where Elmer and Eva Taylor ranched at Rice Creek, across from American Bar; where the best white sand beaches are for camping; where the cliff swallows sing and chitter in Blue Canyon; where Jackson Sundown worked on a ranch near Wapshilla Creek. Sundown was a Nez Perce Indian who escaped to Canada after the battle of the Bear's Paw, in Montana, and reappeared in Idaho a few years later, and who was a world champion rodeo cowboy at age fifty-three, a genuine larger-than-life legend.

I've camped all in all a week of nights on the tiny beach just below the Eye of the Needle, less than a mile from the Snake, and once put my hand ever-so-lightly on a cold, sleepy Western Diamondback rattlesnake coiled among some bunchgrass there. It took me three hard prods with a mullein stalk to get him to rattle and leave. I ruined my right shoulder trying to throw a rock across the river at Billy Creek, though on that last, painful attempt, I made it and thus feel no need to try again. And once, flat water complacent, thinking myself still half a mile upstream, I blundered into the blind-S curve of China Creek Rapid on the ugly wrong side, and nearly made my desperate ferry across to the run on the far left, only to wind up with the raft in a hole so deep there was no horizon but a round wall of froth. The boat inched its way up the hole's bottom, outward edge, but when I cleared the oars it started slipping down again. If we—my wife was in the raft with me—had gone all the way back, where the water piled over the truck-sized boulder behind us, the force of that plummet-rush on the stern would have flipped the raft like a hotcake; my wife and I would have been in that hole underneath the raft then, in the blender swirl of the oars and the round-and-round churn of the water. But instead, I plunged the oars back in and we held there, until the edge of the overflow half-filled the raft, and three- or four-hundred gallons later—five seconds? seven?—we scowed out and washed away like a waterlogged stump.

One night on the beach at Smoky Hollow, I woke up stiff from sleeping on the sand. Sand is a good bed; it will accept your contours; you can burrow down in it and be supported all along your length. But it is hard. Your very weight compresses it eventually to what it is—the offspring and someday progenitor of stone. Anyway, I love sleeping on the beach, despite the occasional large but harmless sand spiders that scuttle over my face, because sleeping there is, in ways only those who frequent country truly empty of extensive human habitation can know, absolutely "under the stars." That night at Smoky Hollow, there was no wind when I woke, though the river's constant wash resembled a breeze through branches and needles. The riffle just downstream from where we camped splashed and plunged. I must have groaned when I rolled from my side onto my back, and that moan let my eldest son know I was at least semiconscious. He was thirteen then, and he said, "Dad, look at the stars." I've never seen anything like the sky that night, before or since; not in the mountains, not in the desert, nowhere. It was close to three A.M.; I checked my watch to be sure. There were, of course, more stars than ever, but it wasn't just uncountable numbers that dazzled us so. It was as though the sky as we slept had come closer, had closed in on us like some gigantic and curious animal. It was all eyes and personality. I felt, we felt, as close to something like God as we would ever be. There was something enormous around and inside us, and although it seems unlikely, to this day the only thing I can compare it to is intimacy.

The river of my childhood was the Mississippi. By virtue of its immensity alone it was dangerous. This was near St. Louis; there were twenty-six locks and dams between us and river's mouth below New Orleans. It was a river of commerce, plied north and south by a near constant convoy of tugs and barges. It was a river of historical and literary significance. By the time I was fifteen I'd read *The Adventures of Tom Sawyer* and *Life on the Mississippi*, and finally, ultimately, *The Adventures of Huckleberry Finn*. I think I knew even then that the river was a mystical thing, what T. S. Eliot would describe as "a strong, brown God"; that, despite the dams and the commercial activity, the endless string of towns and cities along its banks, it was not then and never would be completely tamed. Though St. Louis and Rock Island and Memphis might pump their sewage into its flow, it was, underneath its mud and muck and sludge, the pure melt of snow from the upper Midwest and from the eastern slope of the Rockies. If it had not yet prevailed, it could and someday it would. But one thought twice about eating fish from its waters; one was understandably reluctant about getting in.

My introduction to western rivers came early in my childhood. I remember, during a family vacation in the fifties, sitting on the rocky bank of the Big Thompson River, below Estes Park, Colorado, and thinking I'd never seen water so clear and elemental, thinking as well that it was a wishful, unreasonably hyperbolic name. There was nothing "big" about it. I remember on another trip, high on a rock overlooking the upper Rio Grande, in southern Colorado, being stunned by the view: this pearly flow, supplemented here and there and there again by other equally perfect streams, all down a green and forested valley, as far as my eye could see. And in my early twenties, having moved to Montana to study writing, I learned that I could watch such rivers, and fish in them, and immerse myself in their icy flows, far longer and far more regularly than I could read anybody's poems.

Because I was a lover of maps, I studied mine and came very close to memorizing western Montana: the Clark Fork, the Bitter-root, the forks of the Flathead, the Kootenai, the Yaak. The Mississippi of my childhood had its tributaries too. The Missouri itself, from its headwaters just east of the Continental Divide in Montana, entered the Big River barely twenty miles from my home; the Ohio came in a hundred miles south. But every kid thrashing his way through a social studies or geography lesson knew that. What other waters were there? Why could I not say then—why can I not say today?—where the Meramac joins the Mississippi?—where is the Illinois?—where is the River Des Peres?

And I thought, when I moved to Idaho in 1977, that it would be like western Montana all over again: mountains and rivers, mountains and rivers, if not without end then beyond anyone's ability to experience. But I was wrong. Despite its plenitude of mountains, Idaho is far more a state of rivers than Montana is, which is to say, it is a geography dominated not so much by massive ranges and broad valleys, but by its rivers and their canyons: the long hook of the Snake, from its Yellowstone headwaters and its curl south and west across the southern part of the state, to its hard, westward turn into Washington at Lewiston, may be the most formidable. The Snake is, however, to its glory and misfortune, Idaho's Mississippi, much of it imprisoned by dams. For me, it is the Salmon, the entire system of it within the confines of this one state that has been my home for most of my adult life, that signifies, that characterizes, that sums up the place.

Much of this significance comes from the fact that the river is free-flowing, but there is also the character of the land it drains: most of the largest remaining expanse of undeveloped land—wilderness, we call it—in the lower forty eight. There is no other river like this one anywhere in the nation, outside of Alaska, and for this reason it seems to me that the Salmon is not simply the soul, the heart, the truest, purest bloodline of the state lucky enough to contain it, it is the remnant soul of the nation itself, a country so blessed by rivers that we must have thought, we European makers of civilizations, that they would never end and, thus, by our ignorance or enthusiasm, our greed or desperation, we proceeded to inflict ourselves and our damages on them all, even this one, one of our last, and truly one of our holiest.

For me, the Salmon River was, in the beginning, like most western rivers I have known, not much more than scenery: spectacular, painfully beautiful, here and there pristine. It was scenery, until I entered into it, until I moved at its pace along its canyon lengths, until I knew its rhythms, until, like Twain's riverboat pilot, I could begin to read its text. Now that I knew a few things about it, about its last fifty miles, at least (that old homestead where the pear trees still produce perfect, wormless crops in late September; that grotto a spring creek runs through, of overhanging, honeycomb wheels of columnar basalt, where ferns grow out of the rocks and it stays cool even when the Cougar Canyon air hits 110 degrees or higher); now that I know what little I know, I take great comfort in my enormous ignorance. I could spend every remaining day of my life floating these fifty miles of river, walking the shores, exploring the hills and the side canyons and flat, sandy bars, and never know more than a shred of all that the river could tell me. Twain's riverboat pilot suffered from his knowledge. Knowing the river's shoals and sandbars and snags was necessary, but the knowledge brought with it, well, knowledge. And by such knowing, a good deal of the mystery, and the beauty, was gone. Twain was a writer not often wrong, but about this he was surely somewhat mistaken.

My father is of the generation of men who fought and won World War II, a generation that came of age just as human technology made the jump to apparent warp speed. If he remembers as the first miracle of his life the neighbor lady's simple, white Frigidaire, he remembers also when airplanes were rare; he remembers battleships and carriers, as well, and the bombs that brought on VJ-Day. And so it is my father, like many of his generation, who was a young man—a young father—enamored of the accomplishments of men, of the things they could build with their wits and their hands. On those annual two-week forays into the mountains of Colorado or the hills of Kentucky or Tennessee, we invariably drove, often many miles out of our way, to visit a new dam. I think the idea of it, the fact that someone, somewhere, knew where to start, how to do it: how to block the flow of an entire river! He would exclaim and praise, and no doubt we, his children, were suitably impressed. A dam is an awesome, even an awful, thing to behold, to enter, as we often did. I remember feeling the thrum of the turbines rumbling up through the concrete and being aware of the terrible power there. There was nothing mankind could not accomplish in those days, nothing American know-how could not improve upon. To believe so is hubris, of course, the fuel that fires tragedy. It is a little-known fact that the U.S. Army Corps of Engineers (Edward Abbey called them "khaki-shirted little beavers") has plans for dozens of dams along the forks of the Salmon River, should anyone ask them to start building again.

What Huck Finn loved so much about the river was the escape it provided him—from the stultifying dullness of ordinary life, as well as from the awful horror of human hypocrisy. Huck thought of himself as essentially worthless, of low birth and inclined by blood and temperament toward laziness. He loved to loaf. He was in awe of the grand power and status of the steamboat pilot, and he saw only too late the terrible lie behind the barbaric gentility of the Grangerfords and the Shepherdsons. When he escaped again and again to the river with Jim, they were borne, ironically, ever deeper into slave country, even as Huck was hauled ever deeper into his own soul.

Here at the mouth of the Salmon River, as elsewhere along its length, the sweet lull of its music hypnotizes. It encourages indolence; it can sing you to sleep. I have spent long, lovely minutes awake and dreaming inside its melody; inside the reach of its spell. Once, way up the South Fork—above where the East Fork comes in from over toward Yellow Pine and Stibnite—I saw a spawned-out Chinook salmon floating in a back eddy pool. It had come hundreds of arduous miles from the Pacific Ocean, past the gill nets and the hungry seals and the dams. I wanted to honor it there, to say a few words over it—eulogy, poem, or prayer. But as quickly as words occurred to me, they fattened up, clumsy and maudlin. Anything I said, I understood, I said for me. Never write a poem, Richard Hugo advised, about something that ought to have a poem written about it. I remember I felt foolish, but still I couldn't bring myself to walk on, so I found a comfortable rock and sat and sipped from my canteen and ate an apple. Afterward I lay out across the rock and fell asleep, or at least I think I did; I might have.

Likely it was the sound of the water that brought on the vision, if that's what it was. I was one long muscle. I was swimming, unburdened by extraneous bones, freed of my cumbersome appendages, my legs and arms. I could hardly see, such was the speed at which I moved. By my merest flex and flash, a dazzle of rock shot by below. There were clouds of froth and clouds beyond the froth. The light was blue-green and bottomless above me. It was not so much that I entered the new, blue water, but that it entered me, a perfect ice in my brain. I was on fire with it, rushing, going back through what I'd been to what I had to be. Sweet sun and Jesus river, I leaped, to see the light or clear a stone, I do not know. My skin glistened; it took my breath away, until I entered again the froth and current, a froth myself, a splash and a myth.

That was long ago. I am at the mouth of the river now. My legs, so long crossed beneath me, tingle bloodless. This is how it goes, vision or half-vision in the sound of mountain water. Something startled me. I'd be staring at the water, or at the sand, or at the air itself, when I heard it—a stone rolling over in its bed, a fish. And now I look up and let the light come back, then find my pencil where it has fallen, and begin to write what the river says to me.

To be honest, I hope that ruined shoulder of mine is an even less macho, ego-driven enterprise than it might have seemed. That is to say, I was fairly sure I could throw a rock across the river at Billy Creek, before I even picked one up, but as I have done all my life, I made a silent wager with myself: if I made it, it meant something real; it meant something that mattered to me far beyond distance and arc and muscle. I remember this particular instance perfectly. The rocks I threw that day might as well have been petals from some mopish lovelorn's daisy. She loves me not, she loves me not, she loves me not. Pert near, my grandmother used to say, but not plum.

Of course, what I wanted was to believe in love myself, or to believe in myself as someone capable of and worthy of love. It has just this moment dawned on me, as I think about the river and the times I've spent on it and near it and in it: I have become who I am near rivers, and if I never really loved the Mississippi, it was because I could never give myself over to her entirely. Entering a river requires abandon and luck and faith. It can kill you as easily as a lover can break your heart.

Fool for love that I was, and hope always to be, I found myself that perfect, unimprovable stone, river-round, of the heft of half a baseball. I remember I kissed it, and my cohort thrower laughed. I must have closed my eyes then and come near to meditating; I would have tried to let all the power in my body swirl up from my right leg on a fierce, quick trajectory through my arm. I know I groaned when I let the rock fly. There was a tiny explosion between my collarbone and scapula, a harsh rose of pain, but I knew, when I saw that rock take to the afternoon air, that this one would make it all the way. And when it hit and bounced among the stones on the opposite shore—clack-clack—I remember I nodded, and smiled, and walked straight on into the cold, welcoming river.

ARROWHEAD

to my children, an essay, as an explanation of Idaho

Foolishness, to think it could be explained anymore
              than Massachusetts or Maine. But know this:
that its boundaries, like theirs, are imaginary and political.
              That it resembles Montana and spoons
its eastward front thereto is, in truth, mostly incorrect,
              or that it imagines itself what it was,

which was, before it was, almost no one's
              but the ravens', who outnumber its people
even today. What has come to be
              known as Utah is a growth upon its rump,
or it is, upon Utah's narrow head,
              a tumor fed by methamphetamine, beer,

and the Church of Latter Day Saints.
              That I have never known a Mormon
I did not like immensely, except certain senators.
              This can be explained. It is history.
That Idaho has in its history elected
              senators of considerable greatness,

but not for a long time, not, at least,
              for most of my life here and none of yours.
That the state is an embarrassment and a joy.
              It has been dragged into the century
before this one now well under way,
              its notions of liberty circumscribed

by fearful ideas of stricture and malignity,
              usually religious, which in this republic

have not, will not, and cannot be explained.
That its rivers are among the purest
and most beautiful in the same republic.
That it was established by the republic

it hardly seems to want to be a part of anymore.
That it has a town called Dixie
and a river called the Secesh, short
for Secessionist, but also a Yankee Fork
of the Salmon, and that the Salmon is its greatest river,
named for a noble anadromous fish

most wild examples of which are gone from it.
That this is in part the fault of the republic
it once prided itself on belonging to.
That it is not universally but all too abundantly
racist. Neo-Nazis and Confederates
walk its occasional streets believing Hawaii

is a nation on the continent of Africa.
Its huckleberries are unparalleled,
its mountains spectacular, and deer
are its most numerous citizens.
Some of its human citizens would rather
deer vote than anyone who is not white.

That television was invented here,
for which the state will neither be given credit
nor forgiven. That at its least elevations
the temperature will reach 120 degrees
every summer, and at certain of its summits
the snow, until recently, never went away.

That its hot summer afternoons are indolent
        and perfect, winter nights cold
and often ridiculous with stars. It lies
        athwart the Rockies, it is desert and peak,
tundra and valley, prairie and canyon and forest.
        Its beauty can afflict you like a virus.

That much of its populace is poor and that it is
        determined to keep it that way. That it is
for sale and boasts more millionaires
        per capita than any other state.
That its potatoes are peerless and most
        Americans cannot place it on a map,

believing it must, like the other "I" states,
        be Midwestern, and that is a good thing
in many ways. That its name means nothing
        but scans the same as Illinois, where
I was born and one of you were,
        which can be explained, though Illinois cannot.

That Idaho, like all the other states, is history
        and toil, that massacres occurred here too.
That most of its people are kind,
        like most people everywhere. That I have
for most of my life been in the employ of it
        and been made to feel all the while

something very like an enemy of the state.
        That for some reason I cannot leave,
though my own parents are aging or infirm
        many miles away. This can be explained
but not to my own satisfaction. I feel filial guilt.
        Two of you have happily left the state

already and the other aspires to. That of
          the forty-two people named Robert Wrigley
in the republic, I am the only one in Idaho.
          There are probably more Wrigleys in Chicago
than Johnsons in Idaho. That Chicago
          cannot be explained. There are 242

Dick Johnsons in the nation, five in Idaho.
          That the name Dick Johnson consists of two
euphemisms for penis, and that such
          a diminutive as Dick, when your surname
is Johnson, can in this way be explained. That nothing's
          in a name and wild roses are even now

budding out everywhere around me. There is
          a domestic rose called "Crepuscule,"
while these are wild and called "rosa woodsii." That one
          of you is named Jordan, a name your mother,
when she was pregnant with you, spotted
          on a lawyer's office door

in Salmon, Idaho. That you are the only
          Jordan Wrigley in the republic, that your
older brother is one of only five Philip Wrigleys
          and that Philip Wrigley was one of the richest men
in the nation the year of my birth. As for Jace,
          the youngest of you, he is the only one

anywhere—thus once you were all the only Philip, Jordan,
          and Jace Wrigleys in Idaho, as I am the only Robert.
This can be explained, this too is history,
          which, like the boundaries of Idaho,
is imaginary and political to the extent
          that every polity is a political construct

and therefore imaginary, with the force of law.
        That law is itself imaginary and if not
universally agreed upon nevertheless occasionally enforced.
        There was, until overturned, a law forbidding
a man marrying another man here, or a woman
            another woman. And there was once,

and not all that long ago, a law forbidding
        the marriage of a Mormon to a non-Mormon,
also one forbidding the harvesting of fish
        with electrical current or dynamite.
That this, all of it, can be explained.
        There are cedar trees on this mountain

older than Chaucer and pine trees older than Whitman.
        That the state, though it might claim otherwise,
does not care for schools and teachers.
        That in its Platonic way, the state
also does not much care for poets,
        and that in this regard it is like the others.

That the only true city in Idaho has a river with trout.
        That the state's trout should be foregone
for the trout of other places, and that this
        is explainable and entirely selfish of me.
That sometimes the moon risen
        over the mountain summit to the east

can bring me almost to tears. The most
        beautiful place I have ever been is here,
and I would pin-point it for you
        but not in this particular document,
lest others, in light of my selfishness, should go there.
        That I do not understand this impulse

to explain that which cannot be.
        It is possible you might have been
better off, had you been raised elsewhere,
        though I do not think this is true,
beyond certain measures economic and cultural.
        There are things that cannot be explained

are vastly superior to those that can.
        This document is in some way my form of prayer,
and I pray most often to certain trees.
        Seeing a mountain lion when you are alone
in the woods is a terrifying benediction.
        I hope you remember the afternoon

we watched from our porch above the river
        twelve bald eagles circling in the sky above us.
The sound of a wolf howling is a miracle
        many in the state would exterminate.
That it seems I cannot help myself.
        As one of you has said, living in the state

is like living in an abusive relationship:
        there is always the hope it will get better.
A woman once said to your mother
        raising children in this place is child abuse.
That we understand ourselves to be lucky somehow.
        There is a place we hunted for arrowheads

and hunting for arrowheads is illegal.
        We did not know this, and I found a white one.
We were lucky. A man came from upriver that day,
        walking along to shore to reach us.
"How's it going?" he asked, and I told him we were
        hunting arrowheads and extended my hand,

the white one in my palm. He looked away,
          out over the river. "Hunting arrowheads is illegal,"
he said. He said, "No, what you're looking for is flint."
          That guns outnumber people here
is the pure product of America, which is crazy.
          That allusions are how writers congratulate themselves.

Arrowheads are made of flint: quartz, obsidian,
          jasper, or chert. That making an arrowhead
requires two tools, a hammerstone and a billet,
          usually antler. Also enormous patience and skill.
There are likely thousands in that place along the river,
          lost among chips, fragments, and pebbles.

Today I am in the little building I built
          almost entirely by myself, though each of you
helped me some. That what I mean to say, is that
          love is undertaken, and borne, that it is
beyond explanation and not worth living without.
          A snail's glister trail across a leaf

is a beauty that might be transmitted
          but not explained. That I have met
every governor of the state since I've lived here,
          save one, who was interim and is now
a senator, about whom the less I say the better
          (cf: lines 15-20 above). That sometimes

when I'm fishing I understand a cutthroat trout
          is more distinguished than any man
who ever lived, certainly me. That I am by turns
          misanthropic and generous,
and this is something I might explain.
          That I have been awakened in a one-man tent

173

by the howl of a wolf, that I have been
        awakened in a one-man tent by a bull moose
splashing in a mountain lake, that I have been
        awakened in a one-man tent with a desperate
need to pee, and that soon I stood peeing
        at the edge of camp and looked up to see

a bear risen man-like on its hind legs—
        it seemed hypnotized by a swirl
of yellow butterflies just above its nose.
        That it ran when it saw me there.
It leaped a fallen log as gracefully as a steeplechase
        thoroughbred and made no sound at all.

That the central Idaho wilderness
        is where God lives, which is to say, nobody.
That the central Idaho wilderness is larger
        than many eastern states. That Connecticut
cannot be explained. Nor most especially
        Rhode Island, not being an island at all.

That according to current actuarial charts,
        I have just sixteen more years to live in Idaho.
That I have found two pounds of morel mushrooms
        this spring, and on one mushroom hunting trip
I also found a perfect whitetail buck's skull,
        with smooth antlers not the least gnawed by mice,

and later on, in the same draw, I saw a doe lick the caul
        from her newborn fawn until it rose
unsteadily and followed her into the brush.
        That the Nimi'ipuu called this part of what is
now known as Idaho "Tat-Kin-Mah," meaning
        "place of the spotted deer." That Tatkinmah

is also the name of the property owners' association
        of which I am a member in good standing.
This can be explained, it is meant
        as homage, it is history. It is also
a species of historical rapaciousness
        that makes me uneasy. That I like to walk

the woods at night, because it is impossible
        not to be a little frightened by the dark.
There are very few darknesses in the republic so deep
        as those we may seek out and abide in here.
The man from the electric company
        thought I was crazy, when I asked

that the dusk-to-dawn yardlight be removed.
        That by darkness I mean nothing metaphorical,
and that by metaphorical darkness I mean
        such darkness as is universal, historical, and political.
Also that the measure by which I love hating money
        is the obverse of how much I like having it.

That "In God We Trust" is on our currency
        and this can only be explained ironically.
I do not know what liquidity has to do with money.
        This is something I wish I could explain.
The song of the brown-headed cowbird
        is sweet and liquid, and the many-noted

call of the meadowlark makes me entirely glad.
        The bugle of a bull elk is ethereal,
and the scream of a mountain lion
        primal, and once at a bar, given the choice
of being killed by a grizzly bear
        or dying in a head-on collision, I said

bear, and this is explainable. I am now
        recovered from such romantic nitwittery.
Your mother would rather sleep outdoors
        than in, and that her elegance mystifies
those who know this mystifies me. That for me this is
        only explainable in terms of Idaho.

That the female great horned owl's hoo
        is deeper and more masculine-sounding
than its mate's. Years ago I glanced up
        from a page to see out the window
a bald eagle, holding its place in the air,
        in the midst of a snowstorm on the Clearwater.

It was most surely not the case it turned
        to look at me, though it seemed to,
before it slanted and soared back down
        to the river. Sometimes on my walks
along the shore, I used to lie next to the shallows,
        just so that I could see how the current

in the middle was several feet above my head.
        That I have killed a dozen rattlesnakes
for straying into the yard you played in,
        and that I have skinned one and hung its skin
on the wall above my desk, for which I will not be forgiven.
        Once I found a dead calf moose

so festooned with ticks it looked scaled
        instead of furred. That I have found
nearly every animal in these parts dead, except the raven.
        That I have imagined myself dead
in the woods and not been dismayed by the thought.
        That, as you know, I collect bones

and make widgets and bird perches from them.
          This spring there has been a raven
who likes to sit on the porch rail of my shack,
          and I thought for quite a while
he was watching me, before I realized
          it was his own reflection that fascinated him.

The fascination of birds is magical.
          When the deer here are fatting up
in the fall, I can hear them chew
          the withered, nutmeg-smelling dry blossoms
of the shrub called ocean spray.
          That in winter I will often have an apple

with my lunch and toss the core
          toward the usual two or three does
who take shelter in the thicket just west of the shack.
          There are fewer people in this vast imaginary
polity than in the miniscule borough of Manhattan.
          That all of this is meant as explanation of here,

this place, which is called Idaho, green and golden,
          and I am in the mercy of its means.
Fern Hill Road is a scant twenty miles
          from where I sit today, on Moscow Mountain,
and these few acres where I am are called mine,
          upon which—I tried to count them once—

there are more than four hundred trees.
          They are red fir, juniper, aspen, and hemlock,
but they are mostly yellow, or Ponderosa, pine,
          and the wind in this yellow pine forest
sounds oceanic though it's miles from the nearest sea.
          These yellow pines' millions of needles

are reeds, they are literal woodwinds, a thousand-acre
                weather-breathed bassoon. That it seems
what is most beloved in Idaho is what is also most resented:
                that it is America, and American. This
too can be explained; it is history, which is political.
                That everything American is political,

even its trees: the immense cedars older than Chaucer,
                these hemlocks and pines. Seconds ago
an enormous crack of thunder came, though the sky here
                is clear. The storm is out of sight,
north of the mountain, but as its hard wind comes on,
                it sounds like no other wind in the world.

And that, my dears, may not be true, but it can be explained.
                That unlike me the trees here know only here
and do not hear their music. The wind
                is bound for Montana heedlessly
and without knowing how or why. The sky
                is its apolitical upper state and one of its clouds

can weigh more than one of the mountain's Chaucer-old cedars.
                There is a mathematical formula
to calculate the weight of clouds, but there is no formula
                to measure love (not even mine for you, though
it seems more than the planet itself) nor for this place,
                where I have, as we say, put down roots.

Know that this is a metaphor, as the state, being both imaginary
                and literal, is in some ways as well, in which case
Idaho is Idaho, its pan and handle, its forests and mountains,
                its deserts and canyons and rivers,
its metaphorical backwardness and its literal encirclement
                of the largest expanse of wild country

remaining in the lower republic: that this is why it is what it is,
           and where you have each, in your time,
come of age, as I did too, but belatedly, a grown man,
           midway through the first half of my life:
I'd fallen asleep on a long, flat shelf of stone on the edge
           of a high mountain lake and awoke to see

three coyotes watching me, no more
           than twenty feet away, wondering
if I might be dead or dying, probably hoping so.
           I opened my eyes and there they were.
Wind riffled their fur, their black noses twitched.
           When I lifted my head they ran away,

and when I rose to a sit I saw a trout seize a fly
           from the surface of the shallows
just as the reflection of a many-tonned cloud passed
           overhead. This is simply what happened,
but it may also be why. I fell asleep on that rock
           because I was exhausted from the hike in.

I had never been so weary in my life before.
           I was alone and very lonely, only one
of you was yet born and he was still a baby.
           Nevertheless I vowed that you, then you, then you,
would see and know such things as these in your lives,
           that they might be a counterweight

against the other, outer, imaginary and all-too-real
           nowhere such a nowhere could survive in.
Just remember: that in another history, someone else was here.
           That some mountain lakes and certain rivers
are hardly different now than then, when someone
           shaped this perfect white arrowhead from quartz.

ACKNOWLEDGMENTS

"The Weight of Arrival" first appeared in *The Northwest Review.*

"Seeing Arrowhead, Seeing Flint" first appeared in *Fourth Genre.*

"Under My Skin" first appeared in *The Georgia Review.*

"Of Failure and Shadows" first appeared in *Shenandoah.*

"The Gift" first appeared in *Fogged Clarity.*

"Soul Singing" first appeared in *The Blood Orange Review.*

"Nemerov's Door" first appeared in *The Missouri Review.*

"Arrowhead" first appeared in *Blackbird.*

"The Music of Sense" first appeared in *The LimberLost Review.*

"What the River Says" first appeared in *Five Points* and was reprinted in *Written On Water: Idaho Writers on Rivers,* edited by Mary Clearman Blew and Phil Druker, University of Idaho Press, 2004.

"Who Listens But Does Not Speak" was first presented as a craft lecture at the Palm Beach Poetry Festival, in January, 2014